SAGE was founded in 1965 by Sara Miller McCune to support the dissemination of usable knowledge by publishing innovative and high-quality research and teaching content. Today, we publish over 900 journals, including those of more than 400 learned societies, more than 800 new books per year, and a growing range of library products including archives, data, case studies, reports, and video. SAGE remains majority-owned by our founder, and after Sara's lifetime will become owned by a charitable trust that secures our continued independence.

Los Angeles | London | New Delhi | Singapore | Washington DC | Melbourne

Advance Praise

Indian wisdom and value systems are one of the most amazing and fascinating strong foundations of knowledge. It's really commendable to see that Eastern thoughts are blended in this book, which facilitate the integration of knowledge, application, experience and practice on the Indian corporate playing field. This book is going to be one of the very interesting collections for any student, learner, practitioner, thought leader or even for researchers for any kind of reference at any point of time in their life. I wish the authors great success with this book. I see the practical use of this book in my own research as a really handy guide, whenever I look for management of change.

Dr Rajeshwari Narendran, *Professor, ML Sukhadia University and Director, Academy of HRD, Ahmedabad, Ex-President, ISTD*

It was delightful to read the book *Alchemy of Change: Managing Transition through Value-based Leadership*. Both the authors, Dr H. N. Arora and Rajan Sinha, are scholarly practitioners. They bring in the text their deep insights to explain various issues pertaining to organizational change. Their deep familiarity with Indian spiritual traditions and value systems has been brought to good use. This can be of considerable value to Indian scholars and those in other countries. Their 'Indian Model for Driving Change' is a valuable addition and can be useful for researchers and practitioners. The model has the potential of expanding itself into a larger treatise. The simple and lucid style of writing makes the reader enjoy the text. It is a unique combination of information and wisdom.

D. M. Pestonjee, *Chair Professor, School of Petroleum Management, PDPU, Gandhinagar and Ex-Professor, IIMA*

Rare book on change management where the authors have shared their actual experiences of facilitating change through three case studies, related them with global literature on change theories and ultimately presented change model specifically relevant for Indian culture. A must read for business leaders, human resource professionals and scholars with interest in change management.

Dr Arvind Agrawal, *Partner, Global HR Lead Partners LLP, Former President Corporate Development and HR, RPG Enterprises and President, National HRD Network*

Arora and Sinha have put together a useful compilation of case studies and practical examples from the industry. This approach makes the book a valued reference even for experienced HR professionals. The book provides a refreshing perspective, devoid of stereotype and cliched description. Instead, they have leveraged their legendary thirst for reading Indian scriptures and history and have provided a uniquely balanced viewpoint. I feel this book will be a treasure trove not only for the students but also for seasoned HR practitioners.

Dr Aquil Busrai, *Aquil Busrai Consulting, Former Director HR in IBM, Shell Malaysia and Motorola*

The change has been the lifeblood of human kind, who has evolved over thousands of years from amoeba to chimpanzee to *Homo sapiens*. These changes transform not only the organization but the leaders themselves at many times.

The authors, through their in-depth research, bring out a plethora of change practices that seem to be set amid a spectrum of several solutions, provide a coherent yet diverse perspective and create a successful alchemy for change.

This is a must read book for entrepreneurs and business leaders as well as students, who understand that quite often change management is like a process of metamorphosis that drives leaders and teams to pass through a valley of death with courage, determination and resilience.

Prof. K. K. Sinha, *Dean, Executive Education, BIMTECH, Former Director (HR) NTPC, Reliance Energy, Jindal Steel and Power Ltd*

Alchemy of Change is indeed a labour of love. It is a product of brilliant combination of academic erudition and professional exploration. Arora and Sinha have narrated in this volume a few Indian corporate 'change stories' and how they fit, not fully though, in the conventional (Western) theoretical framework of change management. The book captivates readers with fascinating stories, insightful anecdotes and useful theory frameworks. The authors have been courageous to view transition management, based on their rich 'personal corporate experiences', from a different lens of native wisdom. They have suggested and argued for, quite powerfully, an Eastern Indian model of managing a sustainable transition for well-being of all stakeholders. This is surely a seminal contribution. Change implies giving up the old and adopting new ways of thinking and doing. This book fulfils this statement, quite well. Very readable and stimulating work.

Dr V. P. Singh, *Distinguished Professor, Universities and Ex-OD Advisor, Patanjali Ayurved*

The need to understand and respond to change, in this ever-evolving world, will always remain a contemporary pursuit. Heraclitus had aptly observed that change is the only constant. On this vital aspect of leading change, the authors have endeavoured to blend Western thought with Eastern wisdom, particularly Indian values, with examples that illustrate and insights that illuminate, which are easy to understand and are practical in application.

Dr N. S. Rajan, *former Group CHRO and Member of Executive Council, Tata Sons and erstwhile Global Leader of People and Organization Practice, E&Y*

Change and its management is inevitable in 21st-century organizations. The authors present the art and science of it in a very lucid manner in this book. They underscore the significant role the mindset and culture (both within the organization and outside in the society) play in this often chaotic journey. Indian leaders, who are either starting on or in the midway of a change journey, will hugely benefit from the authors' deep expertise shared through this very context-focused book.

Navaneet Mishra, *Country Manager, Hexagon Capability Centre India Pvt. Ltd, Hyderabad*

I appreciate and acknowledge the immense passion and in-depth, insightful transition process objectively captured by the authors together with more than eight decades of impeccable corporate professional expertise, conceptualising a new paradigm shift to successful change management using Eastern philosophy and aligning with Indian culture.

I admire their efforts in sharing life's learnings with authenticity, practicality and honesty. Culture and values have been thoroughly evaluated with greater relevance to the traditional beliefs of the very essence of Indian philosophy hitherto untapped in management practices. I am personally aware of immense keenness, extraordinary efforts of the authors, great research instinct, voracious readership and great spiritual maturity in their thought process with conviction. Practical industry examples, both in public and private sectors, have been extensively referred to judiciously.

I feel extremely proud of the authors for believing, showcasing and creating awareness amongst knowledge- and guidance-seeking professionals, academicians, researchers and practicing managers/ business leaders.

L. S. Murthy, *COO, Radiant Technologies Inc., USA*

A few years back, Dr H. N. Arora advised us on change management. He has created a benchmark on value-based leadership that, I'm very confident, will be useful to all professionals in creating hurdle-free change. Chapters and case studies in this book are best examples of transformational leadership where a leader is not blindly followed but respected because of trust-based management aiming at common and collective goal of organizational performance. I'm sure that the book will be beneficial to all leaders and professionals.

Atul Sanghvi, *Executive Director and CEO,*
Cera Sanitaryware Ltd, Ahmedabad

The language we use while shaping change often gets jargonized and becomes daunting. *Alchemy of Change* shows that simplicity of the language creates a pull that makes changes easier and faster.

Abhijit Bhaduri, *Columnist, Coach and Author of*
The Digital Tsunami

ALCHEMY *of* CHANGE

ALCHEMY *of* CHANGE

Managing Transition through Value-based Leadership

H. N. Arora
Rajan Sinha

Los Angeles I London I New Delhi
Singapore I Washington DC I Melbourne

First published in 2020 by

SAGE Publications India Pvt Ltd
B1/I-1 Mohan Cooperative Industrial Area
Mathura Road, New Delhi 110 044, India
www.sagepub.in

SAGE Publications Inc
2455 Teller Road
Thousand Oaks, California 91320, USA

SAGE Publications Ltd
1 Oliver's Yard, 55 City Road
London EC1Y 1SP, United Kingdom

SAGE Publications Asia-Pacific Pte Ltd
18 Cross Street #10-10/11/12
China Square Central
Singapore 048423

Published by Vivek Mehra for SAGE Publications India Pvt Ltd. Typeset in 11/13pt Baskerville by Fidus Design Pvt. Ltd, Chandigarh.

Library of Congress Control Number: 2019952698

ISBN: 978-93-5328-761-0 (PB)

SAGE Team: Namarita Kathait, Shruti Gupta and Anupama Krishnan

To fellow professionals passionate about change management

Thank you for choosing a SAGE product!
If you have any comment, observation or feedback,
I would like to personally hear from you.

Please write to me at **contactceo@sagepub.in**

Vivek Mehra, Managing Director and CEO, SAGE India.

Contents

PART IV
YOUR TOOLKIT FOR CHANGE

PART V
LEADERSHIP: THE X FACTOR OF
SUCCESSFUL CHANGE FACILITATION

PART VI
CULTURE AND VALUES AS
VEHICLES OF CHANGE

PART VII
INDIAN MODEL FOR DRIVING CHANGE

Foreword

Today, all CEOs, CXOs and other corporate leaders are expected to play multiple roles. These include identifying strategies to build the organizational future; managing its current performance; studying changes in the world and identifying new opportunities for business; articulating the vision and values for the company; inspiring people with this vision and values; designing systems, structures and strategies; managing teams; networking to maintain relations; getting new sources of information; making and implementing people policies; representing and managing various stakeholders; developing, retaining and managing customers; ensuring financial performance for the present and preparing for the future.

In the sea of multiple roles, most CEOs and CXOs get lost and stick on to do what they are either good at or what is required for the immediate future than to work for the sustainable future of the organization. Post liberalization, in the last two and a half decades, the corporate sector in India has changed drastically. It has become more purposive, benchmark oriented, competitive and accountable to short-term results and quarter-on-quarter financial performance of the company. Today, most organizations have started setting short-term goals. In the past, an organization was set up to serve a larger cause in the society and worked for larger human welfare. This approach was adopted by most businesses in India such as the Tatas, Birlas, Murugappa Group, DCM group, TVS group, JK Singhania group, Hero Group of Munjals and Larsen & Toubro, and in recent times by HDFC, Wipro, Infosys and so on, which have been sustainable, provided employment grew at a fast pace and made a difference in the society. This is the same across the world with organizations such as Nestle, Johnson & Johnson, Ford and Suzuki. These organizations were founded on strong fundamentals and a strong value system of service to people through their products or services. The leaders at the top constantly reminded the people or employees of their values and vison and focused more on them than on short-term gains. The values of the founders and top-level leaders reflected service to all stakeholders—whether employees, customers, suppliers, investors or bankers—and basic principles of ethics and integrity. A large part of these values was drawn from the Indian culture based on seeing each person as a reflection of God or 'Brahma' or incarnation or mirror image of God. The biggest value was respect for people.

With tremendous changes in our economic structure and availability of opportunities to do business or to earn more money, the orientation of many new businesses has changed or has become different. Organizations are being set up to be built for a few years, get funding from a few financiers, make an IPO, boost its market value and sell the company to someone else. Thus, in the last few years, organizations have started getting set up only to be sold and not for service to people. Service became a tool and money the main motivation. Such businesses survive, but not beyond a point. That is the reason why the percentage of businesses that survive over a decade or two has decreased.

Recently, in a seminar on leadership, one of the keynote speakers proudly announced that she created a record by staying with the same company that she joined 18 years ago. She said that she is proud to be so loyal. She went on to say that she did not need to change the company but experienced that her company kept changing every four to five years. The company was bought and sold a few times and every time the name changed, the culture changed, and she played a variety of roles without having to change the company. I know of my friends and students who set up companies to be sold a few years after they made a mark. I also have had students who stayed with the company they started and went through ups and downs courageously as they had started the same with vision and values.

As quoted by the authors, the ET500 survey revealed that 82 per cent of the listed companies have either disappeared or declined during the last 10 years. *Businessweek*'s survey of 1,087 corporate directors in 2005 found that 31 per cent of CEOs were fired by their boards mainly because they mismanaged change. By most estimates, 70 per cent of all corporate change initiatives launched in the 1990s failed to achieve their objective and virtually every survey ever since has shown similar results. Having reviewed a large amount of data and literature, the authors indicate that business firms set up without strong foundations disappear sooner. A strong belief system based on service values and culture leads to organizations that sustain several decades and centuries.

According to the authors, Indian culture is predominantly spiritual, with every human being living in a cosmic vision, leading towards high spiritual truth. It does not mean that all the people of India are spiritual. So true is this statement that I am reminded of the two characters that influenced Mahatma Gandhi as a child: Shravana and his devotion to his duty (carrying blind parents to pilgrimage) and Harish Chandra who stood by his word even when he lost all his kingdom, wife and child. Gandhiji learnt to speak the truth, honour one's commitment and be devoted to one's duty. These are values.

In my own work of effective people, I defined an effective person as one who discovers and uses his or her talent for the benefit of other people. Those who serve many people are very effective, and those who continue to serve many even after they die through the institutions they leave behind are super effective people. To be such super effective person means to be an institution builder, and to be an institution builder means transforming an organization through change and to be value, vision and superordinate goals driven.

David McClelland formulated a theory of achieving society in which he outlined that thoughts precede actions or thoughts create intentions and propel us to action. Thoughts are made of language, and therefore language plays an important role in development and sustainability. The language we may like to promote drawing lessons for this book is a language of values and traditions following the spiritual paths outlined by many. Every change must be value driven and meant for the welfare of all. Leaders play a primary role, and value-based leadership is the most desirable aspect for a sustainable and happy future for all.

This book with the three illustrative cases, incidents and a lot of review of literature from ancient Indian wisdom as well as global writers will form an invaluable collection for those interested in understanding and practising leadership and bringing about change to make a difference in the lives of others.

I like to close with immense gratitude to the authors for sharing their wisdom and contributing to this book through practical cases and wise words. This book is a must-read for all managers, CEOs, CXOs, management teachers and students. The book provides insights into the role that values and spirituality play in laying the foundation to manage enterprises and even our life successfully. It helps bring lasting change where required.

T. V. Rao
Former Professor IIMA, Founder President
NHRDN and Chairman TVRLS

Preface

A plethora of well-acknowledged literature by academicians, thinkers and management gurus is available, advocating almost similar processes and sequence for managing change. Their writing has inspired and catalyzed my own thinking; but the experiences that have enriched me tell a different story. The insights gained from the work and study of theoretical framework have helped me carve out an Indian model for driving change and present it before you in the form of this book.

It was during 1996 when Dr Arora had an opportunity of discussing with the chairperson of Mega Corporation about the modalities of his association with the organization. During discussions, the chairperson and managing director drew an honest picture of the state of affairs then prevailing in the company and his need to change the decaying several decades old culture. The group was gradually losing market across its products, and the management was merely a helpless onlooker of the various malpractices which had eaten into the work culture for decades. A brief analysis of the situation is given in Part II 'Experiences of Change'. He felt thrilled with the opportunity and the challenge of handling a major change effort in the last four years of his active service. This was followed by two other change initiatives he became closely associated with. All three cases are given as case studies in Part II, 'Experiences of Change'. The names of the organizations are fictitious to maintain confidentiality.

The success of change efforts at Mega Corporation and Dr Arora's exposure to the basics of change management motivated him to explore the subject further and delve deeper into managing the people side of change, one of the most unpredictable variables that we will ever encounter. Dr Arora started his research work on management of change under the able guidance of Dr T. V. Rao, professor at the Indian Institute of

Management Ahmedabad, and presently chairperson of T. V. Rao Learning Systems.

Change is a constant in every part of our personal and professional lives. Organizations are no exception, in fact, they are witnesses to dramatic changes at remarkable speed. The ET500 survey reveals that 82 per cent of the companies which were listed have either disappeared or declined during the last 10 years. This is not only with Indian companies, but a look at Fortune 100 shows that 70 per cent of the companies declined just in the same number of years.

Businessweek survey of 1,087 corporate directors in 2005 found that 31 per cent of the CEOs were fired by their boards mainly because they mismanaged change. By most estimates, 70 per cent of all corporate change initiatives launched in the 1990s failed to achieve their objective, and virtually every survey ever since has shown similar results. The success rates of Fortune 1,000 companies for re-engineering—the 1990s most popular change fad—were well below 50 per cent, perhaps as low as 20 per cent.

According to a 2013 Strategy & Katzenbach Centre survey on change management, the success rate of major change initiatives is only 54 per cent. The costs are high when change efforts go wrong—not only financially but in lost opportunity, chaos, wasted resources and diminished morale. Initiatives announced with great fanfare see zealous efforts from employees. Hence, it is only logical for scepticism to set in, if they see their efforts and the company's initiatives fizzle out. This subject was further studied by Herold and Fedor examining over 8,000 individuals involved in over 300 changes, the findings of which were published in their book *Leading Change Management: Leadership Strategies That Really Work.* Amongst many things that they brought about, they found that in most cases, it is not one change but many overlapping changes that take place at the same time, and there is a 'need to implement a holistic change model that takes account of both the abilities of those who will be asked to lead and carry out the change and the context in which the change is to occur'.

On the other hand, some organizations succeed spectacularly at transforming their work spaces, styles and culture, thereby rewriting a new story with great flourish. Change in these organizations brings opportunities, challenges and much excitement. So what enables them to effectively execute their intent when the vast majority cannot? What causes an organization to succeed and the other to fail? Although each corporate failure shall have its own set of circumstances related to environment, industry or product, Professor Chris Argyris (1997), of Harvard Graduate School, found a common thread:

> All were staffed by brilliant people who knew what to do. They were right. Yet, when the circumstances changed, these brilliant people failed to see, accept or adapt to these changes. They failed to learn. Any company, which aspires to succeed, must first resolve a basic dilemma: success depends on learning, yet people do not know how to learn.[1]

Everyone is trying to change. Somewhere it is a planned effort and somewhere ad hoc. Somewhere it is vision driven and somewhere it lacks vision or has a short-term vision. Societal behaviours and rigid norms that are adapted in organizations are mostly based on short-term focus with emphasis on shortcuts. Perhaps because of a 'trader mentality', we do not seem to have the patience needed to bring about stable and enduring change and look for cosmetic solutions for immediate profit.

We may be theoretically aware of the process of managing change; still we sometimes find it hard to bring about meaningful change. The most critical barrier to change, in most places, lies in the lack of belief in and passion for change at the higher management level. They may say all the right words in the right places, but deep in their hearts, their conviction for acting upon the intent is bleak. In the 2012 edition of Prosci's change management study, 650 organizations cited ineffective change sponsorship as the number one obstacle to change. This hesitant willingness is a critical void through which even well-planned changes can come crashing down.

It is also commonly observed that senior executives and employees see change differently. For senior managers, change represents an opportunity for the business and for themselves. The employees see the change as disruptive, with the fear of unknown and the possibility of losing what they have grown accustomed to and comfortable with. We do not make serious efforts to bridge this gap by building awareness of the need for change and fail to accelerate people's understanding of and commitment to change. Therefore, un-learning and re-learning are of prime importance. A globalized economy is creating more hazards and more opportunities for everyone, forcing the organizations to make dramatic improvement, not only to compete and prosper but also to survive. If resistance to change is a normal and natural reaction, then resistance should be expected. If resistance is expected, then our planning activities should be designed to mitigate that resistance, but this is where we make most errors.

In many cases, we also find that organizations continue their dependence on yesterday's strengths, which may not be relevant to contemporary business scenario. Most companies do not anticipate the need for change and just react to events, resulting in negative and traumatic responses that do permanent damage to morale and trust.

It has also been observed that many organizations, through downsizing, consolidation, restructuring and so on, have been successful in reducing costs, while certain quality and re-engineering efforts have helped in removing inefficient steps in work processes. Those efforts helped them turnaround businesses, making them more streamlined. It is important to note that such turnaround cannot, however, be termed as transformation or change. Transformation changes the fundamental image of the business as seen by customers and employees and focuses on creating mind share more than market share. Change truly occurs when individuals in the organization begin working in new ways—displaying new behaviours, using new tools, adhering to new processes and adopting new values. Through turnaround, by exerting pressure by almost every modern management practice, employees work lives might change but not always for the better.

Ever since the floodgates of competition were thrown open, we have been shaken and are struggling to cope with the pace and rate of change. We are forced to re-examine various aspects of business and even organizational structures. Leading that effort has been the person on the top. A leader's preferences are likely to be reflected in the style of transformation. All aspired to improve their companies while meeting certain personal objectives. All were blessed with some degree of management and leadership skills; a few were outstanding at both. More interesting than their weaknesses, though, was the formative role their aspirations and preferences played in shaping the change programme. Whatever a company's potential, transformation is doomed to fail unless change leaders, with selfless spirit, release and orchestrate the energy within the organization, with people adopting new values and behaviours.

Peter Senge, in an interview by Fast Company, said[2]:

It is not simply a matter of more resources, more time, more money, more consultants, more efforts or more intelligence. It is not a matter of resources or intelligence. A lot of competent executives fail at producing and sustaining momentum around change. That suggests that something more universal is at work here. The most universal challenge that we face is the transition from seeing our human institutions as machines to seeing them as embodiments of nature. We need to realize that we are a part of nature, rather than separate from nature. The thinking and acting of the past 200 years—nurtured in Europe, accelerated in United States, diffused throughout the world today—is a machine mindset. That mindset directly affects how we see organizations—and, therefore, how we think about creating change in those organizations. If you use a machine lens, you get leaders who are trying to drive change through formal change programs. If you use a living–system lens, you get leaders who approach change as if they were growing something, rather than just 'changing' something. Nature doesn't change things mechanically: you don't just pull out the old and replace it with the new. Something new grows, and it eventually supplants the old. If you create compliance-oriented change, you will get change—but you will preclude the deeper processes that lead to commitment, and you will prevent the emergence of self-generated change.

Almost every company is struggling with the issue of managing change: what to change to and how to change. Everyone is looking for a mantra to respond to the radically changing business scenario.

In most organizations, structural and system changes become increasingly dysfunctional as they ignore the basic dynamics and spirit of human values. Any change process based on techno-economic considerations to the oblivion of human values is bound to disrupt interpersonal relationships within the organization. The truth is that only value-based institutions that evolve from the wisdom of the soil can bring about enduring change. Asian countries such as Japan, South Korea and Singapore have made proper adjustments in the managerial systems to suit the local environment and culture to implement change processes in their business organizations instead of aping Western management practices.

While transferring technology, there is a tendency to transfer some of the managerial practices and systems also on the belief that these management concepts are universal and can be grafted anywhere. Accordingly, popular concepts such as quality circles, re-engineering, downsizing, 5S, kaizen and so on are being incorporated from abroad as potential solutions for meeting the challenges of change. While it may be easier to transfer and assimilate the technology know-how, the transfer of managerial technology is a difficult process because of the cultural variations. The new systems are based on impersonal equations at work, dissolution of traditional hierarchies and emphasis on assumed contractual relationships—all of which are incongruent with the basic grain of Indian psyche, our cultural heritage and attitudes, which, to a great extent, govern the behavioural patterns. The outcome has been management by chaos, crisis and manipulating structures: anything but management of change in the real sense of the term.

There is already an enormous amount of information on areas such as values, change and leadership. There are few books that hold it all together in a unified single framework which can guide action. The problem is not a lack of information or ideas, but a lack of synthesizing vast amount of information and presenting it in an integrated form for practical use. This book, while emphasizing that organizational change needs to be driven by value-based leadership, integrates all the available perspectives on change in one place.

This book has been written over several years. It is an offering born out of Dr Arora's own journey of understanding and discovering the key principles that make for successful change, enriched by the significant ideas and insights on the management of change in academic journals and the writings of management gurus. The book attempts to provide basic knowledge on change, leadership, Indian culture and values, without resorting to jargons and statistics.

We have divided this book into eight parts. Part I has been divided into three chapters. The first chapter explains the meaning and nature of change and how it affects organizations. This understanding is a prerequisite for change initiation. The second chapter helps in understanding the change process in its totality. The third and final chapter describes how organizations are coping with this cascading change in the present era.

In Part II, we briefly review three case studies, all of which are change stories, but in totally diverse contexts and organizational realities. Actual names of the organizations have been masked and substituted by fictitious names, to protect their privacy and reputation. The various interventions in these case studies are discussed appropriately, along with the process of change.

Part III attempts to discuss a blueprint for managing change starting from preparation to visioning to formulating appropriate strategy and structure as well as how to manage resistance and sustain change on a long-term basis. This is followed by a discussion on tactics deployed for successful change in Part IV.

In managing change, the leadership is a critical variable that facilitates or makes change happen. The whole concept of leadership and the type of leader needed for successfully driving change has been discussed in Part V.

Part VI is devoted to the role of culture and values in managing change and the distinctive characteristics of Indian culture and values that could have a bearing on the change process.

The insights gained from the change experiences and study of theoretical framework have helped us propose an Indian model for driving change, a model of value-based leadership. This has been presented in Part VII. In the epilogue, we conclude with our thoughts on the utility of the proposed model and the journey ahead.

There is a flow in successful change efforts. The chapters follow that flow.

Acknowledgements

There are many acknowledgements when a book represents long years of experience and many known and unknown sources of data and learning.

I would, however, start with special and grateful thanks to the person who encouraged me continuously to stretch existing ideas to new levels. I am most indebted to Dr T. V. Rao, Chairperson, T. V. Rao Learning Systems, and Adjunct Professor, Indian Institute of Management Ahmedabad, for his valuable guidance, insights and sustained encouragement, and for agreeing to write the Foreword for this book. Through his life and work, he has taught me the mantra of working with a missionary zeal.

I also express my sincere thanks to the management and the managers of organizations with whom I have worked and who have demonstrated that value-based change is not only possible, but is the only sustainable way forward.

Crystallizing my thoughts has been easier for me with the inspiration drawn from various authors and thinkers I have read or met along this journey. Most of them are featured in the references.

It was wonderful to have Alok Mehta, a senior human resources (HR) professional and Ila Mehta, a communication professional, as my editors. Both jointly performed the task of polishing and refining the first draft of the book. The enthusiasm of my son-in-law Alok and daughter Ila has been reassuring.

While the book was nearing completion, I took the opportunity of sharing its contents with Rajan Sinha, who was closely associated with me while implementing change process in Mega Corporation and was also a great support in the transformation process at AG Corporation. Rajan came out with many useful suggestions. His inputs during various rounds of discussions were so valuable that

I left it to him to incorporate these inputs in the book as a co-author. I appreciate his contribution, especially in developing the 'Indian Model of Change'.

Rajan, as a co-author, also happens to share the proposed Indian Model of Change with Dr Harismita Trivedi of Institute of Management, Nirma University, whose valuable suggestions have been incorporated in the book. My sincere thanks to Harismita.

We would particularly like to mention Ms Namarita Kathait of SAGE Publications for her insightful comments and demands for enriching the manuscript. She has been a constant source of support during the entire process. Thanks, Namarita.

Finally, I would like to express my gratitude to my wife, Natasha, whose support in letting me find my insulated space and time for this work was a huge encouragement.

The book could never have been completed without blessings of the Divine grace. I feel blessed and humbled in His presence around and within.

H. N. Arora

Dr Arora has been my inspiration since the early 1980s in the mould of Dronacharya–Eklavya relationship. Unlike the tragic ending of the original story, he became my mentor and guide since 1997, when I got a call from him to work with him on a major change project. This relationship has only grown since then. He is involved with many change management assignments, including some in which I assisted him. Therefore, when he wanted to encapsulate his learnings after having completed his PhD under the guidance of Dr T. V. Rao, he invited me to be a part of the project I was too happy to pitch in. Grateful to you, Sir!

My wife and partner, Lila, can never be thanked enough for her support and sacrifice for realizing my career dreams.

I would also like to thank all those leaders and stalwarts including Abhijeet Bhaduri, Dr Aquil Busrai, Dr Arvind Agrawal, Prof. D. M. Restonjee, Prof. K. K. Sinha, Mr L. S. Murthy, Dr N. S. Rajan,

Mr Navaneet Mishra, Dr Rajeshwari Narendran and Dr V. P. Singh who took the time from their busy schedules and did advance review of the book.

Of course, I am also grateful to Namarita Kathait and Shruti Gupta of SAGE Publications for their painstaking support and encouragement that has led to this book seeing the light of the day.

Rajan Sinha

PART I

CHANGE IS A FASCINATING KALEIDOSCOPE

CHAPTER 1

Change Is Life, Life Is Change

Mountains are being worn away, rivers are altering their channels,
valleys are deepening. All life is also a process of change,
through birth, growth, decay and death.

—S. I. Hayakawa

In nature, all change processes take place on the foundation of continuity. No change can be perceived without continuity. 'Change is the only constant thing in today's world—Nothing endures but change. A flowing river constantly changes its contents, shape and course. It may look the same but it never is the same. The river is like the world. Yesterday's world is not the same as the world today or tomorrow,' says Heraclitus, the pre-Socratic Greek philosopher. Change has been contemporary to human existence, an ever-going phenomenon. It occurs in every part of our personal and professional lives and is a common occurrence in business today.

Former British Prime Minister Harold Wilson once observed, 'He who rejects change is the architect of decay. The only human institution which rejects progress is the cemetery.' Change is the law of life. Nothing remains the same from one moment to the next. We are older than we were a minute ago, and that minute is gone forever. It is natural for change to continually occur, whether we expect it or not. Change could surprise us only if we did not expect it and were not looking for it.

Change implies giving up the old and adopting new ways of thinking and doing. The present situation has to be abandoned in favour of a future which is very similar yet very different. Change brings a paradigm shift in the organizational performance, giving a new dimension to business processes and significant improvement in productivity. A fundamental assumption of change is that something different is possible, and there is a chance to improve performance in a meaningful way. Change is, thus, a process of bridging the gap between what is happening and what is possible.

Change means dissatisfaction with the old and belief in the new. Dissatisfaction arises when a system finds it difficult to respond to the environmental pressures. Today, new strategies for attracting customers are being formulated, and a new ecology of competition is developing. We are constantly faced with new situations, new relationships and new pressures. In these circumstances, companies need to realign some aspects of their strategy, organization or culture while retaining the others. That is change. It is a systematic, planned and simultaneous attempt across many fronts to fundamentally alter the basic rhythm of a company. Change management can, thus, be defined as a continuous process of aligning an organization with its marketplace and doing it more effectively than competitors do. The consequence of change is to move the organization from its current state to a more desirable, improved state.

The reasons for change could be as varied as the process of change itself. Whether it is through lower costs, improved service delivery, reduced risk exposure, better product, increased revenues or improved customer satisfaction, each change is an attempt to improve performance. While the notion of becoming more effective or more competitive or closer to the customer could be the motivation to change, these goals need to be translated into specific inputs to organizational processes, systems, organization structure and individual job roles. This is how we define the process of change.

Change is not an event, it occurs as a process. Values, skills and behaviours of people do not change based on certain orders or announcement. This can only be achieved through changing the ways in which people think and act in the organization—through altering their mental models and mindsets and needs constant communication, tools, milestones, reminders and rewards. These mental models or mindsets are called 'routines'. These are made up of assumptions, values and beliefs. More importantly, they contain formulas or codes to guide behaviour in specific situations. Since routines create and sustain stability in an organization, change management is largely about changing people's mindsets.[3]

When we talk of changing mindsets or mental models, we try to persuade the individual to give up some of his or her assumptions and beliefs. When this takes place by way of influencing and persuasion, we experience change in behaviour, moving through unpredictable and messy period of transition, and arrive at a desired new way of behaving and doing the job.

Change is as much a part of today's corporate reality as mindless adherence to rules and routines was a few decades ago. The speed of change and uncertainty continues to dominate the scene. It is our customers, our competitors and the market that decide whether to continue or not. In the new regime, managers do not decide the fate of employees, customers do. The company does not close plants or lay off workers; customers do, by their action or inaction. Our needs are subordinated to those of the people for whom we are creating value. This realization is a defining phenomenon of the 21st century, in the sense that it is no longer a thought in the minds of isolated industrialists or businesspersons or policy makers, but it is now a global consensus.

In fact, in a 2002 speech in European Roundtable Conference, General Motor's boss, Morris Tabaksblat, said:

> Manufacturers are no longer able to impose their will on their customers. The era of push selling is definitely closed. Now, we are fairly and squarely installed in the era of pull marketing. It is no longer a question of knowing what we can sell the customer, but of what we can learn from customers about their needs and how we can help to satisfy them.[4]

Change today happens suddenly, unexpectedly and unpredictably. Markets emerge, flourish and disappear seemingly overnight. Countless technologies, industries and markets have emerged and vanished without trace, like photo-films, VCRs, typewriters, pagers, public payphones, landlines, CRT TVs, just to name a few. This phenomenon of disappearance of ubiquitous products is only going to acquire mindboggling proportions. The basic goal of change management, therefore, is to make fundamental changes in how business is conducted in order to help cope with a new, more challenging technology/market environment.

New Dynamics of the VUCA World

Niccolò Machiavelli, an Italian humanist, philosopher and writer, wrote in his book titled *Prince:* 'It must be considered that there is nothing more difficult to carry out, nor more doubtful of success, nor more dangerous to handle, than to initiate a new order of things.' Yes, change is difficult, but for organizations who want to succeed in today's business environment, it is inevitable.

Today's times are challenging our old and established beliefs and ways of working. Earlier, business was for life. Today, it appears that all of life is for business. We are in the midst of the tumultuous, chaotic, ambiguous and often unpredictable changes. Everything around us is in a continuous state of uncertainty. Today's business environment confronts organizations to go beyond the many assumptions they have held of business and governing the business. At the same time, life today is throwing up opportunities for creating new ways of working, new ways of doing business, new relationships and new ways of living, which might lead to more balanced and wholesome approaches to life.

In today's world, speed has become the dominant factor, and we have to race for an ever-moving finish line to always be a step ahead. Nothing can give a permanent competitive edge. The only way we can counter events is to gear ourselves to look at these changes as potential opportunities. Highlighting the importance of speed, Rupert Murdoch, Australian American business magnate, has said, 'The world is changing very fast. Big will not beat small anymore. It will be the fast beating the slow.'

Something somewhere is affecting everybody in one way or the other. The status of work has changed. The old skill sets are getting outdated at an ever-increasing pace and so is the concept of job security. The simplest example is that of the disappearance of typists, stenographers, data entry operators and an army of so-called class-4 employees. Lifestyle, ambitions, attitudes, values, behaviours, family life, work environment, societal norms and so on—everything is getting impacted. Thus, at the individual level, change can give rise to a spectrum of emotions and reactions: fear, resistance, anxiety, energy, enthusiasm, ambiguity, helplessness, challenge, motivation, cynicism and pessimism. Managing these emotions and reactions, the people side of change, is often the most challenging and critical component of organizational transformation. No change initiative can succeed without getting people on board. It is the degree to which they change their behaviours and work processes that will make or break the change initiative. Change management is the process of recognizing, guiding and managing these human emotions and reactions in a way that minimizes the inevitable drop in productivity that could accompany change. Managing these elements and emotions in ways that keep them focused and consistent is the true challenge of change.

CHAPTER 2

Anatomy of Change

Change Drivers

In the majority of cases, the primary drivers of change are the demands of a dynamic market; the arrival of new technology; the rapid movement to a global economy; emergence of new competitors; swing in the economic cycle and a dramatic shift in the behaviour, values, needs and beliefs of consumers. Power has shifted from inside to outside, from corporate planners to aggressive buyers, who have a huge array of choices and can conveniently switch to something better instantly.

External Forces

As early as in 1999, Peter Drucker and Flaherty wrote, 'External forces producing unprecedented opportunities in the new society were in the global arena'.[5] Because of the scope and diversity of globalization, space does not permit a detailed commentary, but many trends are clearly visible that have had a profound effect in reshaping the environment. Drucker and Flaherty further observed that:

> These external forces are rapidly changing the environment in which business operate:

- The same forces that destroyed Marxism as an ideology and Communism as a social system are also rapidly making Capitalism as a social order increasingly irrelevant.
- Complex and diverse global markets are replacing harmonious and distinct markets operating within the confined national boundaries of conventional Capitalism.
- Distribution channels and customer needs are changing globally far faster than technological innovations.
- There is no evidence that government, trade and industrial policies based on economic engineering will produce the results they promise for the global economy.
- Major regional blocks such as Europe, North America, and the Pacific Rim are becoming the key structured units of the global economy.
- Productivity is the new 'wealth of nations'.
- Increasingly faceless rather than face-to-face exchanges dominate global communications.
- Western societies are no longer the centers of economic, political, and cultural gravity.
- Money and information know no fatherland; they transcend geographical units.
- The rise of transnational corporations, international regionalism, and supranational agencies, has substantively and qualitatively diminished the concept of national sovereignty.
- Competent management, investment, and education are the main keys to economic development.
- The increasing number of new national states is a reaction to the rise of ethnic tribalism throughout the globe. This trend further reflects the superficial geographical demarcations of a world without accepted borders.
- Cross border alliances, both formal and informal, are the strongest integrating forces of the world economy.
- The distinction between the domestic and international economy has ceased to be a reality; however, political, cultural and psychological elements tenaciously cling to the idea.

- Money flows are economic destabilizers, unlike information flows, which have benign economic impacts.
- A business that wants to do well will have to be competitive internationally. Even if it is not in foreign operations, it must have a global mindset.
- Money has slipped its leash; it has gone transnational. It cannot be controlled any longer by nations, states, not even when they act in concert.
- In every developed country, traditional workers making and moving things will account for only one sixth to one eighth of the workforce in the coming generation.[5]

In addition, technological changes such as the internet, mobile telephony and so on have made the gig economy a viable proposition for both organizations and workers. The introduction of artificial intelligence (AI), machine learning, 3D printing and automation is making nearly half of the jobs either extinct or close to extinction. While every technological innovation has also spawned completely unthinkable new jobs, it is difficult to predict the nature of many new jobs that will arise.

These external forces might also include global or local regulations, inflation, cost of living, the economy, court decisions and so on, where we have no direct control. In fact, on developments such as cryptocurrency, even governments will have no control. Changes in these areas have a direct bearing on the business of the company.

Internal Forces

Many a time, internal forces may also cause change to occur. These internal forces might include the following:

1. In terms of Kouzes and Posner's framework, two of the five leadership practices are challenging the process and visioning. The top management may conceive and develop a new shared vision of a new desired future and direction to grow the organization.

2. An organization may be failing to achieve its objectives in key areas of performance such as quality, market share, profitability, growth, productivity, customer acquisition and retention, employee attrition and so on.

3. The emergence of gig economy as one of the dominant characteristics of labour markets, changing demographics of employees in terms of both gender diversity and the growing proportion of millennials in the workforce, their differing expectations and so on.

4. Some of the biggest breakthroughs and innovations have come through employees; whether it is 3M's 'Post-it' notes or 'kurkure' snacks for PepsiCo. Often, they are also in the best position to suggest organizational changes, at least operational changes. Japanese companies have institutionalized kaizen and suggestion schemes and so on as a part of organizational culture. Many listening organizations also make use of large-scale interactive meetings such as town halls.

Destabilizing Events

Large-scale change is usually triggered by some destabilizing events, events of sufficient scope and magnitude to create significant disequilibrium in the organization.[6] These destabilizing events vary quite a bit among industries, but in general they fall within six categories:

1. *Shifts in industry structure or product class life cycle:* Throughout the life cycle of a class of product, there are changes in patterns of demand and users, in the nature of required innovation and in the competition. When an industry moves from one stage to another, it almost always involves a period of disequilibrium for companies in that industry. For instance, shifting consumer preference to quartz and less durable watches wiped out HMT with the advent of Titan and so on.

2. *Technological innovation:* Technological innovation can change the basis of competition within an industry. When the basis of

competition changes, there is great uncertainty. Firms that had a sustainable competitive advantage suddenly find that their advantage is gone, or worse, that they are at a disadvantage. The core competencies of the organization are under a cloud. Typical examples include assetless organizations such as OYO, Airbnb, Uber and so on. Satellite-based communication has revolutionized many industries beyond recognition, what S. K. Sharma calls orbit change. We will talk about it in detail in the Epilogue.

3. *Macroeconomic trends and crises:* Significant shifts in national and world economics can change the basis of competition or present challenges to current ways of running an organization. Any of the factors such as oil crises, trade barriers, foreign currency valuation/fluctuations, inflation, trade balances, consumption patterns, capital formation can suddenly alter the situation in which an enterprise finds itself, thus necessitating significant change. This change can also be benign for some industries. For example, rising oil prices made many previously unviable non-conventional energy sources viable.

4. *Regulatory and legal changes:* Changes in the legal environment or regulatory framework, such as the deregulation of telecommunications, trucking, airlines and banking, can create major modifications in the competitive environment. Mobile telephony is a classic example of how regulatory changes brought about a sea change in communications.

5. *Market and competitive forces:* The entry of new competitors into a market may present new strategic threats if they choose to compete in ways different from historical industry practices, such as the Japanese did in the 1980s with automobiles, consumer electronics and copiers. The result is competition that is more intensive, more aggressive and simply better than that in the past.

6. *Growth:* A final force contributing to strategic change is a result of success in the competitive environment—growth. As organizations become larger, their competitive strategies and their organizational principles may bump into the limitations of size. Successful niche players may find themselves

under threat, especially from new and agile players, as they get bigger.

Many a time, the environment may be friendly but the organization may start to decline due to incompetent management or overconfidence and arrogance of past success. This leads to insensitivity to customer needs, reduction in product development and quality and failure to monitor trends in the market. This situation also offers unique challenges for organizational change.

Change in the Mindset

External change is usually obvious and has immediate impact and, therefore, there is no choice but to deal with it in order to survive in business. The need for internal change is often less obvious and usually seems less immediate. It is usually given less emphasis and priority because results are not immediate and seemingly intangible. The fact remains that we cannot meet the challenges of external change without first carefully managing internal change. The real revolution is inside us. On the one hand, it is traumatic; on the other hand, it fills us with enthusiasm. Belief, courage and conviction are essential before we start the change journey. All change management cases look alike, but in reality, each one is unique to the prevalent culture, beliefs and mindsets. Change is a huge mindset issue in terms of how to perceive, think and behave differently, to improve over the past and the present and prepare for the future.

Any internal or external crisis or performance gaps or identification of new opportunities in the marketplace that the organization needs to pursue in order to increase competitiveness may force the organization to embrace change. Organizations benefit from change that results in new ways of looking at customer needs, new ways of delivering service and new products that might attract new markets.

To succeed and thrive in this liberalized era, the Indian industry has no choice but to become globally competitive. Disparity between existing and desired performance levels has to be identified, aligned and optimized. Performance falling below expectations or below aspiration levels is the trigger for organizational change. Unless organizations take radical action, the gap between their expected performance and actual performance will only increase. Somewhere current procedures may not be up to standard while at other places new ideas or technology may be required to improve current performance. Lackadaisical ways of handling things in a protected environment have to yield place to dynamism, alertness and enthusiasm, to deliver maximum value to its customers by offering world-class products and services at lower costs, with minimum response time. In a market economy, no organization lives in isolation—it has to understand the changes sweeping the business world, and to change itself fast so as to not be overtaken by change but be in a position to take control of its future. Any complacency will sweep them off their feet.

Today, we are into a single economic system drawn by globalization. Each company will have to understand the impact of worldwide trends on current and future operations of the company. Every company shall be required to work out a strategy that addresses a globalized market. Each one shall feel the need to optimize learning opportunities through exposure to various markets around the world and reach new customers. Today's highly competitive economy does not permit us to continue with long-held strategic assumptions and conventional wisdom. We shall have to unlearn, relearn, grow and innovate. Albert Einstein famously said, 'If all you ever do is all you've ever done, then all you'll ever get is all you ever got.'

Art of War, written about 2,500 years ago by Sun Tzu, teaches us to rely not on the likelihood of enemy's not coming, but on our own readiness to receive him; not on the chance of his not attacking but rather on the fact that we have made our position unassailable.

The speed of implementing change in organizations is emerging as a new competitive differentiator. When faced with such turbulence and disequilibrium, we will need to look for new ways to generate and nurture new types of competencies that are more relevant to the situation. Today's digital revolution has impacted how products are designed, manufactured and distributed. Digital technology is today applied to more and more functions of business and we use countless software to lower operating costs, creating better products and improving the business model. It is not a job to be done overnight. It requires deep convictions, enormous upheavals, a vision of what lies ahead and perseverance even at times when we face serious roadblocks and find ourselves in difficulty.

To remain competitive today, organizations must respond to continuously increasing changes in how they conduct business, use technology, involve employees and deal with customers. The fast and ever-changing environment calls for a different set of tools and techniques to manage and administer. Organizations cannot be just endlessly managed based on yesterday's rules, assumptions and practices as they are no more relevant in today's fast-changing environment. If the organizations do not keep pace with the changing technology, consumer preferences and effective business processes, they are bound to lose their competitive edge. John Lilly, American philosopher and writer, has emphasized the importance of change saying, 'Our only security is our ability to change.'

Nature and Types of Changes

The nature and type of a systematically planned change depends upon the need of an organization based on the environmental impact it faces and its prevailing culture. At times, a few transitional changes might be sufficient to yield desired results, but sometimes the organization might need fundamental and radical changes.

Strategic versus Operational

Strategic change is concerned with broad, long-term and organization-wide issues. It is about moving to a future state, which has been defined generally in terms of strategic vision and scope. It would cover the purpose and mission of organizations, .

their corporate philosophy on matters such as growth, quality, innovation, values concerning people, the customer needs served and the technologies employed. It is a change in the content of the company's strategy, covering its scope, competitive advantages and synergy. Operational change relates to new systems, procedures, structures or technology, which will have an immediate effect on working arrangements within a part of the organization.

A typical example of operational change could be implementation of SAP across the organization or addition of downstream product line, whereas an example of strategic change could be Hero Cycles' foray into motorcycle manufacture.

Developmental versus Transitional

The concept of developmental change is based on natural growth, namely, the business organizations change through a predictable growth process like a child to adulthood. Developmental or continuous change builds on the past, without rejecting it. Here, the focus is on immediate impact on quality, quantity, unit cost of production and timeliness through new systems, procedures, structure or technology. Just like the improvement of billing procedures or payroll processes.

Transitional change, on the other hand, is reactive and defensive in nature, adopted by companies that have been successful but find it difficult to compete and thrive in the new environment. In this type of change, the company adopts proven formulas and protects long-established practices to stay competitive. However, it could be more difficult and painful. It is the same change that is brought by acquisitions, mergers and restructuring.

Continuous versus Discontinuous Change

In any change process, the organization continues with certain critical aspects, discards dysfunctional aspects and acquires certain new features. Continuous change, which is incremental and slow, and discontinuous change, which is rapid and radical, both consist of different features and require different capabilities and skills for their management.

In continuous change, the transformation is relatively consistent with what has happened before; we build on the past without rejecting it, namely a development or an extension rather than a radical redefinition of things. Here it is an ongoing process, and we adapt to it constantly, without great efforts. The continuous change model is based on the concept of a current state, a future state and a transition state, and the change is expected to occur over a finite period of time. This type of change can be delegated without intimate involvement of the top management, who need to only facilitate, monitor and support. Here, the expectation is that the move to the future state shall be completed.

During the last few years, we have seen many significant changes in the technological, sociocultural, competitive and political conditions. To sustain growth and profitability in such a fast-changing environment, incremental and continuous change is not enough for most companies today. *They do not need to change what is; they need to create what isn't. This is discontinuous change.* For example, when mobile telephony moved from voice communication to add data communication, and as both voice and data communication become virtually free, there is a sea change not only in technology, but in sales and marketing, revenue models and so on. There are additional challenges with further changes in technology such as VOIP, WhatsApp-based voice communication and so on.

Discontinuous change occurs when the environment undergoes some radical shift, a changed paradigm. This is not an extension of what has happened before and involves radical transformation of the whole organization, discarding most of the past. Since the objective is to bring change in all parts of the organization, its strategy, formal and informal organization and people, it requires the destruction of some elements in the current system. In the words of Picasso, 'Every act of creation is first of all an act of destruction.' Here the cultural issues are felt much more strongly, and there is a great deal of concern with what would happen to existing relationships, power structures, people, systems, positions, channels of information sharing and so on. Because of its multiple initiatives, depth and scope, this usually takes more time, anywhere between three to five years, depending upon the nature of change and the complexity of the organization. It involves multiple transition states, which may even be distressing, painful and demanding on the organization and its people. Sometimes it may not even get completed as short-term goals, which look very attractive, shadow the long-term objective of change. In such a situation, new issues gain priority, necessitating change managers to readjust their initiatives and redefine their objectives during the process of change. It cannot be delegated, and must be led by the chief executive officer (CEO). Given its scope and depth, leadership becomes a necessary and critical element for success.

Incremental versus Radical Change

The size of change has important ramifications on the change management strategy. Just like in boiling frog syndrome, where a frog rather dies despite continuously rising water temperature instead of jumping out, as compared to a situation in which it immediately jumps out of, it is put in boiling water, people adjust to incremental changes without significant resistance, whereas radical change is most likely to invite significant resistance. It is, therefore, necessary that the organizational leadership needs to ask itself on the gap between current and desired state and the degree of departure from the current state before formulating a change management strategy.

Although we have listed different types of changes above, these distinctions are getting blurred in the present era. The speed of change, particularly in the digital field, is so high that the organizations need to be constantly embracing changes that would have been classified differently, in order to survive and grow. It is increasingly becoming debatable, for example, whether a change is strategic or operational, or continuous or discontinuous.

CHAPTER 3

Changing Organizations

If you don't like change, you're going to like irrelevance even less.
—General (Ret.) Eric Shinseki

India's largest automobile company, Tata Motors is a classic case of how the group reinvented itself.[7] They were predominantly manufacturers of commercial vehicles. Shrinking of Indian commercial vehicles market by 40 per cent led to a loss of ₹5 billion in 2001. This shook them up and they decided a three-phase six-year recovery strategy. The first phase focused on stemming the bleeding, followed by the second phase aimed at consolidating their strength in India. The third phase planned to expand internationally.

In the first phase, they brought down the break-even from two-thirds to one-third of capacity utilization, so that they would not incur a loss even with 40 per cent shrinking of market. This was done with the massive induction of information technology (IT), apart from other things. The second phase concentrated on bringing out new products suited to the Indian market to fire up consumer imagination. Nano was one of the results of this effort.

The third phase included Tata's acquisitions and tie-ups across the globe from Tata Daewoo in Korea, to Spanish bus manufacturer Hispano Carrocera to Jaguar in the UK, Land Rover in the United States, Thonburi in Thailand and so on. Today, they have a robust presence in 50 plus countries, in all the continents.

The same adaptability characterizes the entire Tata group. Founded in 1868, it is not only one of the oldest groups, it has operations in 80 countries and is recognized as the 13th most innovative company in the world, besides being India's most-admired business group.

In 1997, Netflix disrupted the entertainment industry by offering monthly rentals to customers so that they could avoid late fees payable in their previous arrangements with traditional rental companies. With the advent of YouTube, the way customers consumed video had changed. Netflix survived and beat the market again in 2007 by offering streaming services.

HMV reinvented itself by packaging its library of thousands of songs into a radio-like digital product, Saregama Carvaan.

Survival of the Most Adaptive, Not the Fittest

The emerging world is a world of competition and *the basic philosophy now is the survival of the most adaptive.* Organizations, therefore, trying to sustain competitiveness in today's aggressive markets have to successfully manage internal change for gaining a competitive edge. Although change may be disruptive, organizations feeling the heat of a competitive environment understand that they have no choice. The pain of remaining in the current state shall be more severe than the pain involved in implementing change.

Why have some organizations succeeded while others have failed? Organizations that have learnt how to manage change effectively are continually looking forward, not backwards. They are taking control of the future by regularly evolving new ways of doing business, building new core competencies, creating new markets, bringing out new product concepts and thus continually changing the rules of the competition. This cannot be done unless they are willing to change and move from where they are today.

We are living in a period of major organizational changes. Corporations are significantly downsizing, re-engineering, working out new strategies and processes. During the last one decade, we have been bombarded with a large number of seductive and contradictory ideas for ensuring corporate success in a changing world—total quality management, empowerment, re-engineering, just-in-time, total plant maintenance, kaizen, flexible employment, 5S, benchmarking, self-managed teams, employee stock options plan, voluntary retirement scheme, knowledge management, learning organization, six-sigma, restructuring, design thinking, agile organization—the list goes on and on.

New markets appear while old and reliable ones vanish. As customers have become sophisticated and demanding, the shelf life of products and services is getting shorter. The customer determines obsolescence, not the manufacturer, and this reality cannot be overlooked.

Ever since the floodgates of competition have been thrown open, Indian companies have been forced to re-examine their customer relations, quality parameters, distribution network, technical and managerial capabilities and processes, and organizational structures. With globalization and the consequent integration of economies, there is a greater emphasis on price, quality, innovation and satisfaction of customer needs. They have rather become the guiding principles of competition. Rapid and widespread diffusion of technology, freer movement of capital brought about by a single goods and services tax in the country, increasing focus on transparency and digitization and so on have changed the rules of competition, suddenly forcing companies to expand globally. New systems, technologies and processes have shortened product cycles.

Due to advancement of technology and entry of new tech-savvy millennial generation in the workforce, the softer aspects of the workplace are also being influenced. The way we work, the way we interact with each other, the age-old attitudes and mindsets are being discarded everywhere. Traditional management styles based on rigid hierarchical structures and highly controlled information sharing are ineffective. Instead, a new management style is emerging that is more open, flexible and decentralized.

Any industry or organization that fails to take cognizance of changes around it, such as changing consumer preferences and attitudes and lifestyles, social and political climate, changing employee aspirations, modern technology and processes, has to pay the price. Textile and jute industries in India, which failed to keep pace with the changing times, are classic examples of this syndrome.

Each organization is different in terms of structure and design, technology, work culture, management styles, resources, employee expectations and attitudes, work processes, customer needs and complexities of the operating business environment. A change technique that works in one organization may not work at all in another organization with similar culture and within the same country. Any change, therefore, has to be introduced keeping in mind the people, the complexity, uniqueness and the culture of an organization.

Our management sciences are heavily influenced by Western concepts and practices. While importing technology, we also tried to mindlessly import their management systems. If one system or concept works well in one culture, it is not necessary that it would be successful in another culture as well. Since countries in the West are more advanced, and basic concepts in most cases are universally applicable, total rejection of Western concepts and techniques would be an overreaction. However, it must be remembered that systems and practices are developed keeping in mind the specific cultural needs of the society, and because of the vast cultural gap, outright transplantation of Western management systems cannot (and has not) succeed(ed). We should adopt what is appropriate for us and supplement it with learning, specific to our context and culture. Unfortunately, people often talk about this issue only in clichés.

We should never believe that the changes we have been able to bring about are the end of the journey of change. There is always another wave breaking on the shore.

PART II

EXPERIENCES OF CHANGE

CHAPTER 4

Mega Corporation: Challenging Old Paradigms

The Mega Corporation group ranked among the leading Indian conglomerates, with significant presence across its multi-brand businesses. The group has many modern manufacturing facilities in northern India and an extensive marketing network spread across the country. Mega Corporation has many subsidiaries and associate companies, and competent and path-breaking joint ventures with global leaders.

The Downfall and the Triggers

At some point of time, the group found it difficult to respond positively to the changes in the economic environment. The group's turnover at this juncture was around ₹3,000 crores, with a workforce of more than 15,000. The group was gradually losing market in all its products because of its deeply engrained and stereotypical work culture. The two major products of the group had lost substantial market share during last seven to eight years. In one product, the share came down to 14 per cent from 40 per cent, and in another major product, it came down to 17 per cent from 25 per cent.

The percentage of labour cost to turnover was almost two to four times high, as compared to the competitors. The productivity comparison was no different. It was the lowest in all products, as compared to all the competitors. Labour cost being abnormally high and the productivity very low, the writing on the wall was very clear for the group. It was time for the group to face the reality, especially in view of the fact that many new multinationals as well as domestic competitors were preparing to enter the market soon.

During the late 1990s, the management conceded that the external environment had become very competitive and many international players were in the process of setting up manufacturing units, which promised to produce superior products at reasonable prices. It had, therefore, become imperative to reduce cost and improve quality so that it could face the emerging competition.

In addition to regular workforce, there were more than *3,000 casual labourers*. These casuals had to be engaged against such workers, numbering hundreds, who had not been working at all, being either leaders of the union, ex-leaders and undesirable characters, on whom management had no control. Casuals were also required to complete certain jobs left incomplete by the regular workers or refused by them, being heavy in nature, or required to assist the regular workers either for material movement or for machine operation. In normal course, all these jobs were to be performed by regular workers, but the management was feeling helpless and was compelled to get the job completed through casuals.

In addition, there were hundreds of employees in the category of staff and supervisors who were highly skilled workers in the past but were now promoted based on seniority. Having no supervisory potential and yet being promoted, they were not prepared to work on machines any more. In the process, the company lost them as skilled workers and gained poor supervisors. All such people therefore were almost idle.

Charity, Not Business

Overtime (OT) was another factor that destroyed the work discipline. In spite of over manning and engagement of casuals to the extent of

49 per cent of workers' strength, grant of overtime was a common practice. In fact, it had been the main bone of contention and, many a time, long work stoppages and strikes had to be faced on the issue of grant of overtime. Interesting devices were evolved to create situations whereby grant of overtime became a necessity. There was nothing that the management could do to stop or curtail unwarranted overtime. In case only a few workers were needed to stay on overtime to complete a certain job, they would refuse to stay unless the whole department was put on overtime. Indeed, the charity overtime or industrial peace allowance was necessary for running various manufacturing plants.

Another charity was in the form of *incentive payments*, under various schemes. All the incentive schemes were linked to certain ad hoc and negotiated figures of production and not on industrial norms. These schemes were introduced from time to time, separately in different product divisions to achieve higher levels of production, against negotiated amount, through a table giving figures of production over and above the existing figures and the amount admissible.

Concession given in any plant, legitimate or otherwise, had its immediate repercussions in all the plants of the group. Although all the product divisions were independent companies, with separate board of directors and management, and a few with the joint venture partners on the board, the demands and facilities agitated for and ultimately obtained were similar. Though the management, products, market, competition, manufacturing process, labour cost, business plans, profits and the issues faced by these different companies were different in nature, there was a tradition to have a common settlement, with similar wage and benefits across the group. The union, which was one for all the group companies, never agreed for business-specific separate settlements and benefits. Collective bargaining towards a common package, against an ad hoc rise in production, became the norm. This was being objected to by the foreign partners in many companies, and because of such unrealistic wage structure and costs, a few companies were gradually being driven to closure.

Indiscipline

Indiscipline was rampant and embarrassingly showing the group in very poor light within industry peers. Hundreds of workers, leaders, ex-leaders, undesirable characters, sick and non-performers were not working but drawing full wages, incentives and overtime, as admissible to other workers. In such cases, they even managed their attendance, sometimes, without being present, for days at a stretch. There was no check on late coming, and anyone could enter any time and leave anytime. There were many who did not return after lunch, but it always went unnoticed. In a few plants, even the working hours were reduced on flimsy grounds, to allow the workers to come late and go early. During night shift, all manufacturing units were fast asleep by 2 AM after completing the targeted production. No change in the manufacturing process or shifting of any machine was allowed unless additional money was given.

Neither could any worker be transferred from one place/machine/department/job to another. It was impossible to take any disciplinary action, even for major misconducts, as it would immediately result into work stoppage, and the management would backtrack, under compulsion. Even if a charge sheet was issued for a major offence, and the charges proved, an apology was accepted under pressure from the union and the workers were let off practically unpunished. Dismissal was unheard of. The approach had always been to focus on immediate results and production numbers at all cost, without any consideration of long-term health issues, processes, quality, discipline, final cost nor for the company's repute. There was no fear of punishment and the management was so helpless that sometimes workers even did not pay for tea, snacks and so on for months together and the management could neither stop service nor take any action. No subcontracting of any component was possible as it was feared that this would immediately result into work stoppage. There was a total environment of rowdyism.

The management had *no control over the unionized workers*. Even for allocating machines to workers, it had to seek the permission of the union. The union resisted any move by the management if it adversely affected the interests of even a single member. In case of any conflict between the union and departmental head, the personnel department intervened and tried to find solutions. However, they would end up persuading the department head to agree with the union and advising them to stay in their good books.

One senior government official once remarked that 'the management and control of the company has been contracted to the union and company management has lost the right to manage.'

Managers had lost hope of ever getting an opportunity to manage. The whole cadre either had withdrawn or was frustrated. They had lost faith in the management as it had always backtracked and never held its ground. They felt that they were duty bound to maintain peace at any cost and meet production targets. To achieve this objective, they maintained good relations with the union leaders by appeasing them and used them to solve their problems at the shop floor. Everyone went out of the way to keep leaders happy so that the show could go on. A few managers even started business with the company, directly or indirectly, resulting into various malpractices and supply of poor quality of components/material.

Steering the Change

The chairperson of the group entrusted the task of bringing change to the newly inducted group HR head (change facilitator). Incidentally, there was no focused and clear vision from the chairperson, just some ad hoc statements. In the circumstances, the facilitator had to start the process of change with a broad framework of objectives. Large, discontinuous change in the organization is brought about not just by a single leader, but through a larger set of key personnel who make crucial contributions to the planning and implementation of change.

The change facilitator, therefore, thought of forming a change management team, the core group, consisting of five heads of various businesses, to create a new vision for the group, a compelling picture of what the organization wants to be and where it wants to go. It was the foremost task to carefully craft the vision after taking stock of the organization's culture and its environment.

These business heads were independently looking after their businesses, without any coordination, among themselves, though part of one group. All of them were busy in 'somehow' achieving production targets and trying to fit in as per the boss's requirement. In the process, workers/union were being appeased by extending benefits, creating chain reaction in all the other divisions of the group. These businesses were being run by the respective business heads as their own empires, without any formal or informal consultation or coordination and without any joint responsibility for all the businesses of the group, and thus lacked the pragmatics of a group identity. However, individually they all seemed concerned about the state of affairs and fast-changing business environment.

It was necessary to align the total core group with the singular and dedicated goal of change. The change facilitator personally reached out to all other five members of the core group with a message that the task may be difficult but not beyond reach. It was incumbent on them that they identify a specific set of problems and opportunities, have a common understanding of why and how the environment within needs to improve, and are able to identify, develop, mobilize, align and orchestrate the various in-house sources of energy. They needed an elaborate plan of action to neutralize the sources of resistance.

The focus was on collective efforts of leaders of various business units—the core group. With their management and leadership skills pooled together and used collectively, it was reassuring to know that an appropriate strategy for change and its effective execution was now a definite possibility.

These five top executives, along with the change facilitator, forming the core group of six had a two-day off-site meet to have an honest review of the situation for proper diagnosis and giving a shape to the vision for change and the proposed plan of action. Everyone was fully involved and it was decided to first lay down the ground rules for the functioning of the core group, which included absolute confidentiality, an open mind, mutual trust, transparency, information sharing, regular interaction and staying true to the group's vision.

Taking Baby Steps

The first step in any change process is an assessment of the environment to identify what organizational conditions need change. The core group, therefore, first analysed the situation and then suggested a diagnosis, thereby identifying reasons for the present situation. This was a very honest diagnosis where the business heads openly accepted that they have been only concentrating on the numbers without any concern for managerial processes and not taking cognizance of the impact of their decisions on other businesses.

It was time, now, for the core group to give a greater definition to the purpose, scope and desired outcomes for the change effort. Understanding where we are, why there must be a change, how far reaching it will be, and what the ultimate goal is, are critical components of change process. Having analysed the present situation and completing its diagnosis, the next logical step was to draw a detailed picture of the future, a wide-angle photograph, on a different set of basic assumptions, describing the scope and scale of change and as to how the organization would look like after change. The core group, after due deliberations, took a view on desired state.

Having defined the scope and desired outcomes of the change effort, it was now easier for the core group to crystallize the vision for change comprising elements of a notion of the way the company needs to be organized to make the most of the market opportunity. The core group accordingly finalized the vision, as follows:

To become India's most successful company through world-class manufacturing, right work culture and an environment where energies could be diverted, channelized and utilized for growth.

The core group, moving forward from the stage of crystallizing the vision for change, was engaged in designing the change programme and the strategy. The vision statement laid down the purpose of the organization, highlighted the need for right work culture and gave guiding principles and values. It was now time for the core group to draw a road map to show how to reach the goal.

The approach focused on the development of work culture based on trust and collaboration amongst all employees through change in attitudes, beliefs and values, empowerment at all levels, especially first-level managers and supervisors, and pursuit of a long-term, consistent and fair policy devoid of ad hoc solutions and appeasement. The objective of new work culture would be to unleash and synergize the energies of all the employees of the company towards achievement of common goal and vision.

Unlike the previous settlements, it was planned to use the proposed settlement as an instrument for change in work culture, adoption of industrial engineering norms and new work practices. The basic theme of the previous settlements used to be a certain increase in wages against a negotiated increase in production, which inevitably led to suboptimization of resource capacities and continuation of traditional work practices, resulting in higher labour cost and low productivity.

Traditionally, wage settlements were perceived to be the only instrument of bringing change, and as the existing settlement was due to expire shortly, it was considered prudent to lay maximum emphasis on the next wage settlement. The core group, therefore, laid down the objective of the next settlement. There was realization that it would be difficult to get employees' support for the proposed change in work culture without offering something in return, the group prepared itself for negotiations.

It was considered necessary to develop a common approach to issues such as developing positive attitude, developing managerial and supervisory skills, sharing common vision and values and proper integration of inputs with the transformation strategy. It was, therefore, considered necessary to strengthen training and development activity for need-based inputs to various categories of target groups, namely, top management, middle management, supervisors, HR heads, security heads, union and workers.

Certain preparations were considered necessary to be made before launching the process of change and start of negotiations with the union for the settlement. These included compilation of data on competitor's productivity and best practices, laying down manning and production norms through various studies and benchmarking, developing proper inventory of manpower in terms of skill, age, qualifications and so on, strengthening chain of command right up to the first line of supervision, and finalizing various systems.

One team of industrial engineers and HR specialists was recruited from outside / drawn from other parts of the organization to work full time on collection and collation of these data from across industries, industry associations and so on in all sectors in which the group was operating.

As a critical strategy, the core group thought it was imperative to draw people out of their comfort zones and develop support for the change programme. The need to create a shared vision was given more weightage than consoling those who might be apprehensive towards change. Reassuring those who may be afraid of change may often prevent the process of change and, therefore, it was considered necessary to create a shared vision amongst people.

The first step towards a shared vision was by way of involving the operation heads of various business units, the key people, next in command to business heads. The approach of the workshop for operation heads was participative, making them partners in planning and creating the strategy for change. Commitment to vision or developing a shared vision becomes easier if people participate in planning and implementing the change programme, on the principle that people support what they help create.

In Mega Corporation, the managers felt helpless and had almost lost their right to manage because the union was powerful. It was felt that if these managers, through the change process, could see light at the end of the tunnel, which meets their needs and values, most of them would deal quite well with the change. The top management, that is, the core group members, interfaced directly with the managers of all divisions to provide clarity, initiate a debate and encourage managers to develop their own responses specific to their own business roles. They were encouraged to challenge,

question and learn, continuously refining and committing themselves to the vision and the process of change.

As per the management's strategy, the forthcoming settlement
was the main instrument of change, which had to be negotiated with
the union. With the day-to-day increasing operational pressures,
with liberalization, trade unions are required to find solutions
for complex problems hand in hand with the management. The
union must work as a collaborator and not as an alternative power
centre, especially unions which have internal leadership, as was the
case with Mega Corporation. Collaborative union is best where
union leaders collaborate with the management, retaining their
credibility with the workers, and the workers are convinced that
the management was fair. Mega Corporation's case was altogether
different where the union, taking advantage of management's
weaknesses, had been exploiting it for undue benefits, and the
management had been appeasing the union for decades.

It was, however, time to raise the heat and wake the union up
first. It was necessary for the union to feel the extreme level of
emotional tension before they were prepared to change. This was
possible only through a clear understanding of realities and the likely
scenario if they fail to face the reality and wake up. Accordingly, a
few informal meetings took place with the union for an evaluation
of the business environment vis-à-vis our preparedness to compete.

The union had a key role to play, and it had to be convinced
about the need for change through hard evidence and data. For the
union to share and support the change, it was necessary to analyse
the situation thoroughly. Accordingly, the scenario and all hard-
hitting data were presented to the union leadership by the concerned
business heads. To ensure complete appreciation of the situation
amongst the union leadership, the data included business scenario
vis-à-vis competition, present position of the company and future
business plans. Also embedded in these data was the fact that how
imperative the correction of and cooperation from the workforce
was for the survival and growth of both employees and the company.

*In order to soften the union resistance, repeated communications about the
current situation and imperative for change were also made to first-line*

supervisors in Hindi, which inevitably travelled to workers at large. This helped in building the ground-level perception that change was urgently needed to protect jobs.

Green Shoots

After these meetings, there was a palpable buzz and the feedback was positive and encouraging. Extract from a letter by one senior manager to the change facilitator read as follows:

> It was a real pleasure listening to your down to earth views which came like whiff of fresh breeze—change can never be thrust down on people but has to be faded-in gradually so that enough adjustment time is provided—we have started with uncorking the bottle to release pressure and providing ample opportunities to people to unwind themselves and express their views and concerns. This process has helped them to de-steam themselves of years of pent-up feelings. As a result, many issues have got thrown up which have helped us to do introspection and take timely corrective action, wherever feasible. People have been encouraged to express themselves without inhibition and fear. This is, however, just the beginning and a lot needs to be done. We are confident that with your active support and encouragement, we shall be able to give practical shape to our dream of instilling pride in people to be a part of the 'Mega' family.

Over time, predominance of unions' influence in policy decisions, particularly with reference to welfare and discipline, chain of command had become emaciated with inversion of power relationship at the first level of management. Supervisors and first-line managers used to feel powerless while dealing with workers earlier. Regular communication and training at this level energized these managers and supervisors. Similarly, team-mirroring workshops were held to enhance alignment and trust level between shop-floor managers and HR function. All these efforts led to greater cohesion and unity of purpose in the entire management team.

With core group meetings, training programmes, presentations to the union, and communication meetings all around, everyone started sensing some change in the air. Lots of fears, doubts, suspicions, apprehensions started vibrating in the environment.

Resistance to change does not have anything to do with bad will. It is human nature to resist change. We want things to stay the same, thinking that change will be bad for us. The company faced strong resistance from the workers. There was no reason for the workers of Mega Corporation to support change as they were comfortable in the existing environment. There were work stoppages, strike and breakdown in negotiations. However, with handling resistance at various stages of change, having repeated and focused communication, promoting teamwork and learning culture, practising value-based behaviour, and total transparency, the company could succeed in bringing about change in their five-decade-old culture.

The change brought an end to unproductive malpractices. Improvement in productivity ranged from 30 to 70 per cent, while reduction in wage cost per unit of production was between 10 and 30 per cent. The workforce was reduced by 26 per cent, and overtime payment came down by 75 per cent. All the malpractices related to either discipline or productivity were removed and a transformed, productive work culture was established.

Mission Accomplished

There was a drastic change in the work environment after the implementation of the agreement. Now each worker was producing a much larger quantity than what he produced earlier. All workers worked diligently for eight hours in order to achieve the required output. The management obviously felt triumphant. A new work order had been established and the management had complete control over its affairs. This was also the time to demonstrate that the change brought about is not just for survival but also for growth and a better life. To ensure that the workforce feels safe and see a better and healthier future for themselves in the new work environment, the managers of all the business divisions were briefed by the core group members about the humane side of the management and that the workers need to be handled with a touch of care and compassion.

The memorandum of settlement described the management's and union's *dharma* and statement of commitment. The management called for accountability and performance from managers, involving them fully in solving workers problems. The overall improved performance, as a result of change, helped the company improve its market share and image in almost all the businesses. As reported by a leading business magazine, the company had powered ahead from the fourth spot to the second in the industry in the first five months immediately after the change.

There were indeed a few hiccups, as is perhaps inevitable in such large-scale change. For example, one business head reneged on his commitment and started resorting to old practice of using sops for short-term gains. However, these were minor blips and the group continued on course to greater gains.

The group chairperson mentioned in its annual general meeting that 'the cultural transformation will afford the company greater operational flexibility in resource utilization and higher productivity. The company has now achieved a much healthier business structure and is now ready to attack the markets with new vigor.'

CHAPTER 5

AG Corporation: A Change that Reinvented a Corporation

Established in 1970, AG Corporation is a medium-sized engineering company located in the central part of India. It employs around 450 qualified professionals and skilled workers. The company is accredited with ISO 9001-2000 and is renowned as a specialist in the field, producing international quality products with wide market acceptability.

Besides being a quality producer, the company had a good order book and an immense growth potential. Up until now, it had done very well; however, recently a feeling of insecurity and demotivation had crept in. Employees, including managers, were not paid salaries continuously for three to four months. Sometimes there was no cash available even to meet petty day-to-day expenses. Suppliers either stopped delivering or provided material at their terms. This affected the manufacturing activity as well. In these circumstances, it was only the owner and CEO of the company who stayed determined and strived to find solutions.

He had started this company in 1970 after having worked briefly in a tool manufacturing outfit. He chased his dream and set up this unit to develop quality substitutes indigenously, which would replace imported tools and parts in the Indian market. He gained repute and record for industry-best technology and engineering excellence. For the first five years, he managed to generate good revenues, without borrowings. In due course, the company diversified and, in turn, became the sole supplier to larger outfits.

Having worked closely with people at the shop floor during the initial stages of business, the CEO had a personal connect with each employee and was held in great respect. A God-fearing human being, his compassion and moral standards made him a favourite in spite of his own management style and weaknesses.

With his willingness to experiment and take risks, the CEO's commitment to innovation ensured that the company's products developed through in-house R&D, right from scratch. He believed that innovative solutions were as important as carrying people along, because a strong team is an essential prerequisite for success.

Solitary Reaper?

Ironically, such a firm believer in teamwork had no team to support him. His top team members, of the level of directors, were uncomfortable with his style of functioning, and mistrust was high. The gaps had so widened that all decisions and actions were seen with suspicion. One director felt that the company had tremendous potential but it needed strategic direction and vision which was not forthcoming from the CEO, who was running the business on his personal whims and was not open to suggestions.

Another director also expressed similar views, painting a very dark future of the company, with no hopes of revival, and expressing serious concerns about his own future and that of his family. He was equally bitter about the CEO's style, saying that he was in habit of taking independent decisions and doing everything himself.

Contrary to these feelings, the CEO felt that these top executives do not feel accountable, neglect their responsibilities, do not support and guide their team members, and always look for scapegoats in others, for their own failures. It is under these circumstances that he himself has to follow up the progress and stay hands-on.

In today's fast-changing environment, constant and strategic realignments of an organization's culture, management processes, tools and techniques have become a necessity. So, while the CEO's main focus was on arranging working capital for day-to-day operations, he could never free himself from the manufacturing and commercial preoccupations.

Therefore, he brought in a change facilitator to assist him in the renewal and realigning efforts. Story of this change effort is, in fact, the story of strong sponsorship of CEO and value-based leadership.

Situation Analysis and Corrective Actions

A situation analysis revealed that there was no role clarity, and people did not feel accountable. Information was not communicated and shared, managerial and supervisory cadre was confused and demoralized, and a sense of insecurity prevailed all around. Employee turnover was quite high and workers were dissatisfied over anomalies in salaries. Nothing seemed to be moving without a follow-up from the CEO and the company was being run on a crisis mode on a day-to-day basis.

There was hardly any system for rewards and performance management. Rewards were decided by a few top executives, without involving the respective department heads. This had caused general dissatisfaction among employees.

The situation at shop floor was no different, where the productivity was very low, with material wastage and rework amounting a whopping 40 per cent. Departments such as maintenance, planning and materials created additional bottlenecks for the shop floor. In the absence of reviewing and monitoring processes for operations and performance, almost every activity needed follow-up from the CEO.

The situation analysis established the need for immediate interventions for discontinuous change. It needed a top-level and committed management team for driving the interventions. A substantial time was spent on resolving interpersonal issues with the senior management, which led to fears, suspicions, doubts and apprehensions about each other. Added to this was the absence of communication, which had only widened the gaps. With counselling and face-to-face open discussions with the whole senior management group, bridges began to appear between individuals and the team. Things started looking brighter, a beginning of new trust-based relationship, with transparency and open communication seemed to be getting established.

The CEO and ED, along with the change facilitator, met with heads of departments to share and discuss the change agenda, which consisted of restoring shattered confidence and developing positive attitude through teamwork, focused communication and system support. The company had tremendous potential, and these heads of departments were motivated to take the ownership of the change agenda to bring the company back on track. These meetings later became a regular feature for reviewing and discussing future plans.

The CEO attended regular communication meetings, which had a trickledown effect on the heads of departments, who started sharing information with their respective staff. He even addressed workers sharing the company's dreams, intent and efforts with them.

ED started conducting regular weekly meetings of heads of departments for reviewing the manufacturing performance, looking into bottlenecks and promoting networking and collaboration.

The core group of top five executives started meeting every day for one hour to discuss strategic issues relating to business and operations, take vital policy decisions and monitor their implementation.

Vision, mission and values of the company were finalized through a two-day workshop conducted by change facilitator, with the help of an external trainer, and attended by top management and heads of departments. The strategy to institutionalize them was also worked out and implemented. Teambuilding workshops based on Belbin framework and trust exercises were also conducted for bringing about greater understanding and cohesion in the top team.

Increments and rewards were given through a newly introduced performance management system, with defined roles, responsibilities and key result areas. The process of rectifying anomalies in salaries was initiated.

The organizational structure was changed by defining new roles and accountabilities and promoting the deserving talent.

When the situation looked grim due to instances of neglect or lack of trust, honest and open discussions and counselling were held to tackle the situation.

Sometimes, change efforts would take a back seat either due to day-to-day crisis or due to a casual approach. The delinquents could, however, be brought back on track by highlighting the importance of change for the future of the company and, thereby, their own.

Regular feedback from CEO, ED and others on such issues as incidents of neglect, important developments, behavioural and attitudinal responses, lack of responsibility, coordination, areas of concern and interpersonal issues helped in making timely interventions.

A new agreement was signed with the union, resulting in improvement in productivity, elimination of wasteful practices, laying down new production norms and introducing a new incentive scheme. New work practices such as multi-skilling, multi-machining and so on were also introduced.

An exercise was undertaken for identifying untapped potential in managerial and supervisory staff to help chalk out their career growth within the organization. A two-day outbound training programme on teamwork and leadership was conducted for the top team, while many other need-based programmes were conducted for managerial and supervisory staff. Workers were trained for TPM.

Mission Accomplished

Celebrating success and small wins became a regular feature at the beginning of all monthly communication meetings chaired by the CEO. Top team and managers felt that changes were quite visible in the attitude of people and that things were moving in the right direction. They became optimistic about the future of the company and started motivating people in their departments. The CEO also felt that he has now plenty of time for strategic thinking instead of firefighting and follow-ups and that the company is now seeing smooth functioning and good times after three years.

Today, the turnover of the company is five times as compared to the time when the change efforts started and the net profit has grown 15-fold. The management feels that the organization is prepared to meet any challenge now.

The CEO was open to feedback and prepared to change. He was once overheard saying, 'You cannot change others without first changing yourself.'

CHAPTER 6

Akash Industries: Lip Service Does Not Bring Change

Akash Industries is a large pharmaceutical company located in northern India. Though set up hardly a decade ago, it has evolved into a fully integrated pharma company, with state-of-the-art manufacturing facilities. The company has six manufacturing plants, employing around 5,000 people, with highly integrated portfolio of products for the pharmaceutical and health care sector, with a customer base across the globe including several blue-chip organizations. It has WHO GMP certificate ISO14001:2004 and many international accreditations.

The company is managed under the direct supervision and control of the owner CEO. He is involved in day-to-day decision-making and managing the business quite successfully. The CEO is a God-fearing, compassionate and caring person with high moral values. Having worked closely with people during the project stage, he knew most people personally and commanded great respect from one and all.

He would take personal interest in organizing two family get-togethers each year: on Independence Day and Republic Day. This was a regular feature, attended by six to eight thousand employees and their family members. These get-togethers were loaded with entertainment programmes and a variety of food. The CEO would personally meet each employee and family members and would mix with them in most informal environment, including on various festivals and pujas, a normal practice in the company. Valuing relationships has earned him great respect and fondness by one and all.

During discussions with the change facilitator, the owner CEO laid out his expectations of a corporate culture of excellence, with all systems and policies in place and where roles and responsibilities at senior levels are well defined and where people feel so accountable that he is not required to look into day-to-day issues.

Situation Analysis

The first step in any change process is an assessment of the environment, organizational culture, values, processes, competencies, systems and so on to identify what conditions need to be changed.

Situation analysis revealed that many senior positions at the level of plant and departmental heads were manned by unqualified people who, being old associates, enjoyed the confidence of the CEO. They had been with the company from the very inception and learnt the nuances of their job at the workplace itself. This group had neither any managerial or leadership qualities nor any exposure to the outside world. Some of these senior executives had to be provided with additional staff to operate their personal computers, check mail and send replies, as these executives were not technology savvy. Most of these executives were not fluent in English either, and this hindered their communication with multinational customers. Their leadership capabilities were mostly below average: due to lack of either competency or the organizational culture that did not believe in developing capabilities. The CEO, a dedicated and hard-working person, was aware of the pressing need for developing leaders within the company, but never gave enough attention to it.

The CEO often dealt directly with junior employees in all functions and plants, bypassing the hierarchy and thus creating a communication gap. During meetings the change facilitator had with various individuals and groups in the manufacturing plants, many junior executives mentioned that they reported directly to the CEO as well as received directions from him without the knowledge of the plant head. He himself reviewed the performance of all the plants periodically wherein many important decisions were taken to bring about improvements. However, in the absence of any follow-up mechanism, these were easily forgotten and brushed aside once the meeting was over.

At another level, the CEO used to conduct meetings with senior executives, called 'Mission Excellence', every six months.

People were expected to come out with their free and frank views for improving organizational effectiveness towards ensuring excellence. Besides this, various committees with specific tasks were also formed from time to time, but soon after the first meetings, all these efforts used to fizzle out due to lack of follow-up. There was intent, but no system to support it getting translated into action.

Frequent change in the organizational structure was a common feature. Roles and responsibilities of people, especially at the senior level, were added or discarded by the CEO for reasons best understood by him.

There was no delegation of authority, and each decision was taken by the CEO himself, including approval of small value purchase orders or signing cheques. People at all levels were used to and happy running to the CEO for every small issue. Plant and functional heads had no say even in the selection of managers and staff for their respective divisions as all selections were made by the CEO himself. In the absence of any performance management system and reward policy, the heads could not recommend rewards and promotions of their subordinates. All such decisions were taken by the CEO himself.

Even the postings and transfers of staff in various plants/functions were done by the CEO without any involvement of concerned plant/functional head. There was a general perception that CEO does not trust anybody and wants to keep all controls with himself. Simultaneously, a lot of his time and energy were being spent on unproductive or routine meetings.

Most new appointments made by the CEO had to be terminated for poor performance within a few months of joining, reflecting on his poor assessment of people. Terminations were otherwise also a common feature even for employees who had put in long years of service. People could be terminated for minor lapses or sometimes on baseless reports from those whose major lapses were invariably overlooked. This created a feeling of insecurity amongst all ranks, and everyone was trying to appease the CEO rather than concentrating on their job.

Another important reason for insecurity and high attrition was the behaviour of senior managers, especially the old associates, who being unqualified themselves, could never tolerate a better-qualified person working with them. They saw such people as a potential threat, thereby depriving them of opportunities to contribute and grow. The CEO wanted these senior managers to find support and assistance in well-qualified appointees, but these associates ensured their exit sooner or later. Suffocated in such a frustrating atmosphere and having to report to staunch stalwarts who restricted their growth, fresh joiners would choose to exit. Forty to 50 per cent of these appointees used to quit within 6 to 12 months of their joining. The rate of attrition in senior- and middle-level management was also high as they had no freedom to perform and there was continuous meddling by the CEO. An entrepreneur should choose the right kind of people to do the right kind of job and then step back to let them function.

Workforce assessment was never done, and there was no sanctioned workforce for any department. Overstaffing could be seen in all areas. Extra hands were provided to complete the production targets. Productivity was just 40 per cent of the industry norms.

Interpersonal conflicts and absence of teamwork had become a part of company's culture. There were serious conflicts amongst senior executives who were critical of each other not only during private conversations but also in open forums. These conflicts had an adverse impact on organizational effectiveness. The CEO chose to overlook this important human relations aspect. In view of his direct involvement in and control over all affairs of the company, he probably did not believe in teamwork. People at all levels were individually delivering under fear and pressure.

The production department did not own the responsibility of quality and considered it to be the responsibility of quality control department. Each case of non-compliance with quality norms was referred to the CEO. The focus has always been on bottom line—achieving production targets with least concern for the processes. Inefficiencies, wastages, higher cost, low productivity and bad practices were tolerated for the sake of production targets. These deficiencies had, thus, become part of the organization's culture.

There were suggestion boxes where employees used to put in their suggestions and grievances. The keys of all these boxes used to remain in the CEO's office, and no one else had any access to these suggestions except the CEO himself. However, more than suggestions, it was the CEO's information gathering box. To top it all, the CEO had also posted junior officers in each plant for gathering details on day-to-day happenings and reporting directly to him. These officers would attend all meetings conducted by plants/functional heads and report detailed proceedings to the CEO. Senior executives used to call it the 'spying network'.

The HR department had a poor image, known for not helping the employees, not looking into their problems/grievances and working in a dictatorial style. It was just involved in routine work of record keeping and salary dissemination with no understanding of systems, developmental activities and creating a positive work culture. Threats of being thrown out of the company by HR managers and plant heads were a common feature. HR was perceived to be the most ineffective department by one and all.

Action Plan

To sustain growth and profitability in today's fast-changing environment, most companies need radical transformation of the whole organization, but this was not the case with Akash Industries. It had a satisfactory record of growth and profitability. The need, therefore, was of continuous or operational change relating to new systems, procedures, structures and management processes that could bring greater organizational effectiveness and the company could meet the challenges of the changing competitive scenario and move towards achieving its goal of growth.

Accordingly, a detailed proposal and action plan was developed for the proposed operational change. The action plan included organizational structure; fixing accountabilities; identification and filling up of organizational and operational gaps; potential identification and development; monitoring, review and follow-up mechanism; succession planning; developing new and fresh talent; performance management and reward system; creating a learning environment through information sharing and learning forums; setting up systems in all functional areas; defining roles and responsibilities for all positions; creating a forum of plant and functional heads for cross fertilization of ideas and team building across functions/plants; and finally developing a performance-oriented culture of excellence where people are treated with respect and care and they contribute their best to achieve organizational goals.

The action plan was discussed with the CEO in detail, and it was very encouraging to find that he agreed with all the points in the proposed plan. Detailed proposals were worked out, with strategies for implementation with reference to all areas covered in the action agenda. The CEO thoroughly discussed each proposal, seeking clarifications, arguing, reacting and reviewing alternatives. Modifications, if any, as agreed to after discussions were incorporated in the final draft ready for implementation. The CEO would ask for the copy of the final draft saying that he would go through once again and clear it soon for implementation. The approach paper and draft policies were ready for implementation, covering almost all areas mentioned in the action agenda but no proposal ever got final go ahead for implementation, even after continuous follow-ups and reminders.

With reorganization of HR department, introducing systems and formats for timely actions, making HR managers aware of their role and responsibility, and with constant monitoring and counselling, the image of HR changed and employees felt that they were getting help and grievances were being looked into. There was positive feedback about the new environment in the organization.

Sponsorship Challenge

An effort was also made to implement the new performance management system. The system was received well in the organization as for the first time the managers and senior executives got an opportunity to report upon their staff. The recommendations for increment and promotion were compiled based on these appraisals and given to the CEO for approval. The benefits of the system were discussed with him while handing over the recommendations. The CEO, however, completely overlooked these recommendations, which were based on the data derived from the system, and decided each case based on his personal impressions about people. This was a big setback. This gave a clear message that he himself was scared of change and was only giving a lip service to it.

The CEO once mentioned, during discussions, that he wants systems in the organization but cannot surrender his authority to take decisions. Though being very open to feedback receptive, he would, most of the time, agree to the needed change but would continue with his old style. Many a time, during discussions, he would agree that he was not able to take a stand, correct the situation, manage his time and priorities, and reaffirmed his commitment to change. Somewhere he had a belief that he has been managing so well all these years and that was probably the best style. It is difficult to unlearn behaviour that made us successful in the past. It looked that he was also somewhere scared of making changes fearing that these may prove counterproductive.

Organizations cannot be just endlessly managed based on yesterday's rules, assumptions and practices as they no more remain relevant in this fast-changing environment. We need to innovate and innovation means change. The CEO either did not understand or did not want to understand that companies which aspire to take control of their future need to manage organizational change.

During his 14 months of association with the company, Dr Arora had 22 long meetings on change agenda with the CEO. In all these meetings, he spoke to him logically, rationally, emotionally and sometimes even challenged him. He was a great listener with a cool mind, looking to be a great advocate of change, agreeing all the time to implement the proposals already discussed and finalized; however, these proposals never saw the light of day. Despite the stated change goals, he invariably defended the status quo and behaved as he did before. Any effort to bring any change in existing practices was resisted.

Finally, all the gains dissipated and the company reverted to its earlier ways of working with added cynicism in the minds of everyone that 'nothing will change here'. If the CEO does not apply to himself what he has been sermonizing, then the whole process of change is bound to break down, as happened in Akash Industries. The only consequence of failure of planned change is to set up an organization for more painful and calamitous change, brought about by inexorable march of market forces and technology.

We love routines and, by being apprehensive about possible adverse consequences, do not try anything new. What we forget is that in today's fast-changing scenario, problems and new challenges can gatecrash any time and we could be caught napping if we have not prepared the organization to meet these challenges.

PART III

MANAGE IT OR BE READY FOR OBLIVION

CHAPTER 7

The Blueprint

There are a hundred reasons why change can be daunting. Despite well-laid-out plans, few things turn out as planned. No one can predict with accuracy how the trenches will behave. Nilakant and Ramnarayan (1998) say that this is so 'Because real change in real organizations is intensely personal and enormously political. It involves altering not only an organization's strategy, structure, and operations, but also the perceptions, expectations, and performance of thousands of people.'[8]

According to Prosci, 'simply coming up with right solution is not enough to ensure that the results are achieved.' The right answer alone does not:

- Create buy-in
- Create commitment
- Mitigate resistance
- Eliminate fear
- Ensure compliance

Change management, at its core, is a structured approach for bridging the gap between a great idea and tangible value to the organization. Therefore, it recommends 'balancing effort between developing the right technical solution (arriving at the right answer) and applying change management (crafting a solution for managing the people side of a change)'.

Managing the time period between the current and the future state, when the change process is under way, is a monumental task. This is the phase of high uncertainty as the status quo gets dislocated during this phase due to a wide range of change interventions and the future state does not become operational. Handling this phase is, thus, a gigantic task.

Steps for Successful Change

There are no universal rules or well-defined sequence of steps for managing change. Each organization, based on its history and culture, faces unique challenges and exhibits specific strengths and limitations. Irrespective of the background, culture or history, a major organizational change does require a sequential approach to change. There have been many prescriptions, with well-defined sequence of steps, from well-known behavioural scientists and management teachers.

Tichy and Devanna[9] define change as essentially a three-phase process. The first phase is 'awakening', where the organization becomes aware of the need for change and acknowledges that the status quo is no longer viable. They call the second phase as 'mobilizing', where the organization creates and adopts new structures, procedures and people to move the organization in the new direction. The final phase has been referred to as 'reinforcing', where the organization absorbs the new behaviours, attitudes and practices into its culture.

John Kotter (1996), in his book *Leading Change*, mentions eight steps that are essential for successful change[10]:

1. The entire management must communicate with one voice that there is no alternative to considerable change.
2. A group of executives with enough power and flexibility should be set up to lead the change effort as a team.
3. People need to know where and how they are going. Therefore, a credible vision and strategy has to be crafted.

4. All means must be deployed to communicate it to all the stakeholders.
5. People at all levels need to be empowered to facilitate change.
6. Opportunities for creating short-term wins need to be created lest critics and cynics spread negativity.
7. Use short-term wins to undertake bigger changes. Systems and processes that come in the way also need to be modified/changed.
8. Stabilize new changes by top management personifying the new approach and connecting it with corporate success.

We have refrained from enumerating different models of change, including Kurt Lewin's (unfreezing–refreezing) and so on, for simplicity. One more reason for not including the widely popular Kurt Lewin model here is that, in the present era, in a typical organization many change efforts may be overlapping, and it may be unrealistic to imagine discrete states of unfreezing and refreezing.

However, a counter-proposition that most such programmes are guided by a theory of change that changes in attitudes lead to changes in behaviour is fundamentally flawed. 'In fact, individual behavior is powerfully shaped by the organizational role people play.'[11] They believe that:

> Individual behavior is powerfully shaped by the organizational role people play. The most effective way to change behavior, therefore, is to put people into a new organizational context, which imposes new roles, responsibilities and relationships. This creates a situation that, in a sense, 'forces' new attitudes and behavior on people.[11]

The aim of these overlapping steps is to build a self-reinforcing cycle of commitment, coordination and competence, and the focus is on reorganizing employees' roles, responsibilities and relationships to solve specific business problems.

Based on practical research conducted in more than 900 organizations, Prosci has given the ADKAR model, which is an acronym for Awareness, Desire, Knowledge, Ability and Reinforcement.[12] It is a goal-oriented model and focuses on the actions and outcomes required for change. It emphasizes that organizational change occurs only when each person is able to transition successfully and focuses on five actions and outcomes necessary for successful individual change, and therefore successful organizational change.

In the ADKAR model, the process is sequential. It emphasizes that each step must be completed before moving on the next, as it is not possible to achieve success in one area unless the previous action has been addressed. The five sequential steps of the ADKAR model are as follows:

1. *Awareness* of the need for change: Understanding why a change is necessary is the first key aspect of successful change. This step explains the reasoning and thought that underline a required change and answers some basic questions such as what is the nature of change, why is the change happening, and what are the risks of not changing to the individual and to the organization. In the absence of such awareness, the natural reaction will be resistance to change. Prosci's benchmarking studies show that a lack of awareness is the greatest source of resistance to change.

2. *Desire* to participate in and support the change: In this step, individuals are able to reach a point where they make a personal decision to support the change and participate in the change. Building desire is achieved by addressing 'What is in it for me?' and 'What is in it for us?' regarding the change. A desire to support and be part of the change can only happen after full awareness of the need for change is established.

3. *Knowledge* on how to change: Successful change requires knowing how to use the new tools or perform the new skills after implementation, and knowing how to change. We should list the skills and knowledge needed to support the change. In addition to formal training, other methods of transferring knowledge such as one-on-one coaching, mentoring and so on might be useful. Two types of knowledge need to be addressed:

knowledge on how to change (what to do during transition) and knowledge on how to perform once the change is implemented.

4. *Ability* to demonstrate the new skills and behaviours: It is possible that employees may understand the change on a theoretical level and even have the knowledge to make the change but ultimately cannot demonstrate the required skills and behaviours. In this model, ability is understood to be the difference between theory and practice. Barriers inhibiting the ability need to be identified and employees need to be supported through practice, coaching and feedback.

5. *Reinforcement* to sustain the change: The final element in the ADKAR model is reinforcement, a critical step to ensure the change is sustained. Ensuring that changes 'stick' and individuals do not regress can be achieved through positive feedback, rewards, recognition, performance measurement and corrective actions. Reinforcements that will help in sustaining the change should be listed, and it must be ensured that there are no opposing incentives to the change.

All these approaches lay down general principles with some differences in terms of emphasis. Somewhere the focus is on developing the right attitude and mindset towards change, while in another approach the emphasis is on implementing change at the business unit or plant level. The ADKAR model focuses on individual change and ensuring that each person makes the transition. Since the model focuses on the individual, we are able to measure the ground realities and steps required to assist them.

While models of change management are useful, in that they describe the general principles that can help us understand and manage change; the change rarely follows the exact steps these models suggest. If a change followed an exact pattern and was predictable, there would not be any need for different models. While we can make use of basic steps that are essential to follow and that are common to organizational change, we should go about implementing change based on unique characteristics of the culture and history of an organization, and the environment in which the organization operates.

Qualities of Change Agent

Sometimes, especially in a large organization, one person may not have all the qualities of a change agent. In that case, more than one change agent with complementary capabilities may perform the role as an orchestra.

If you are the change agent, check yourself:

1. Are you a good empathic listener? There is a lot of debate on what constitutes empathic listening. Dr Brené Brown provides a very succinct four-point framework[13]:

   a. Perspective taking: ability to take the perspective of another person and recognize it as her or his truth
   b. Staying out of judgement
   c. Recognizing emotions of other person and
   d. Communicating that you understand without 'silver lining' it

2. Are you flexible and open? While goals may be specific and may be time bound, a change agent has to find creative ways to accommodate concerns of different stakeholders without losing line of sight of goals.

3. Do you have knowledge of change management principles, experiences of other organizations in similar contexts, both within the same industry and in other industries, technology involved, project management, government regulations and so on. The wider the knowledge, the better equipped you are.

4. Do you have full support and confidence of the top management?

5. How are your networking skills? You will be required to form critical coalitions of key influencers.

6. Are you able to withstand strong mental and physical pressure without losing calm and composure? Do you have sufficient physical and mental energy, which you will be required to draw upon? Are you generally optimistic?

Change management can be a very exacting job. As we have discussed Rosabeth Moss Canter's analogy elsewhere in the book, change, like the transformation of a caterpillar to a butterfly, can be a very gooey sticky mess in the middle with most people wondering whether it was worth it.

7. Are you generally seen as trustworthy across different stakeholders?

8. Are you an excellent communicator, both spoken and written, including in the language spoken by the masses in the organization?

CHAPTER 8

Preparing for Change

It is important to remember the wise saying of Kōnosuke Matsushita, who founded Panasonic, that when you change your point of view, your results also change. In other words, the process of change begins in the mind, with a belief that change is necessary. To begin any change process, we must first start by understanding why the change must take place. The management of change, therefore, starts with a sense of discontent with the current situation and articulation of a vision for the promising future. The challenge, therefore, is to analyse the business and market environment, agree to a compelling and distinguishing vision, set up relevant goals and values, and bring people, technology, finance, business and support processes closer, to enable the company to fulfil the needs of its various stakeholders.

The organization has to rediscover itself; it has to have a relook and modify the underlying assumptions and inconspicuous premises which form the basis of its decisions and actions. We need to challenge the status quo, the beliefs, values, attitudes and consequent behaviour, which currently define it, before we can build up a new way of operating. 'Every organization must be prepared to abandon everything it does to survive the future,' says Peter Drucker.

Unless we know what is to be changed, it is of no use to know how to set about making the change. The size of the gap between the desired state and the current state explains the need to change.

It is necessary to be aware of where we are before starting work on where we want to go. An organization has, therefore, to look into its past in the context of the present and the present in the context of the future and assess whether it can continue doing the business the way it has been doing.

Before we start the process of change, irrespective of its nature or type, we should be conscious of current practices, processes and culture that may hinder the success of change project. Organizational culture and value system play a vital role in how an organization reacts to change. Keeping this factor in mind, we can pre-empt certain reactions and plan accordingly. There might be certain groups or individuals resisting change, given their cultural predispositions. Plans will have to be prepared accordingly to handle these reactions. Organizational change signifies leaving behind a traditional culture and climate of conformity and creating a new culture that allows innovative ideas. Not paying due attention to various aspects of existing culture and value system and not planning for these obstacles in advance might lead to incomplete solutions.

Change involves moving from the present state to a future state through a transition. There has to be clarity as to what the organization needs to change and how it should go about it. This calls for an awakening, which requires a frontal assault on the status quo so as to arouse the emotional energy of an entire organization. This energy could manifest itself as fear but has to be converted into personal commitment to a plan of action, which would be the only fuel that could sustain a revolution.

Jack Welch states that facing reality is crucial in life, not just in business; you have to see the world in the purest, clearest way possible, or you cannot make decisions on a rational basis. Facing reality means dealing with what all of us would prefer to avoid: danger, failure and our own shortcomings.[14] Such an audit should include the assessment of performance, policies, practices, core values, attitudes, management style and strategy. The current state of the organization should be evaluated against the performance of other organizations from similar industry, especially its business competitors. It helps the organization to identify gaps and issues that need to be addressed. Such benchmarking enables the promotion of a compelling need to change, and the performance gap, and the consequences of failure can be clearly understood. Just the key performance indicators need to be benchmarked against the best practices in the industry. Possible courses of action can then be identified and evaluated, and a choice made of the actions for the journey to the desired state.

Content of 'What' and Process of 'How'

Both content and process are important in managing change. No doubt, 'what' we want to do (the content of change) is important, but 'how' we do it (the process of change) is even more important. Process is as important as the product of change. The contents of organizational change are technology, marketing, quality and cost, while the process includes strategy, structure, systems, policies, methods, attitudes and other HR practices. For most of us, the goal is so fascinating and tempting that we sometimes lose sight of the details altogether.

Swami Vivekananda, emphasizing the importance of means, has said:

But whenever failure comes, if we analyze it critically, in ninety nine percent of cases we shall find that it was because we did not pay attention to the means. Proper attention to the finishing, strengthening of the means, is what we need. With the means all right, the end must come. We forget that it is the cause that produces the effect; the effect cannot come by itself; and unless the causes are exact, proper, and powerful, the effect will not be produced. Once the ideal is chosen and the means determined, we might almost let go the ideal; because we are

> sure it will be there, when the means are perfected.
> When the cause is there, there is no more difficulty
> about the effect; the effect is bound to come. If we
> take care of causes, the effect will take care of itself.
> The realization of the ideal is the effect. The means
> are the cause; attention to the means, therefore, is
> the great secret of life.[15]

Andrew and Richard[16] state five conditions required for any planned change and adaptation to take place:

1. Leadership has to put change management as a top management agenda.
2. Appreciation that people alone make the change happen.
3. People must be aware that there is a need for change.
4. Strategy should be clearly spelt out in actionable terms.
5. All members of the management should be aligned.

This model shows that the scenario planning can be a major factor for change. We shall have to understand the nature of change, its type, size and its impact on people. Some people may face very little change affecting their day-to-day work while for others change may involve doing something entirely different, and doing it differently! We should be prepared to assist each group in the best possible way and plan accordingly.

One of the essential prerequisites while preparing for change is establishing a high enough sense of urgency in managers and employees. Communicating a sense of urgency keeps positive energy flowing. Without a sense of urgency, people become complacent and do not put in extra efforts and make the needed sacrifices, things so essential for change. Top managers have to demonstrate a sense of urgency in their day-to-day behaviour with the belief that radical change is possible. They must assess the organization's strengths and weaknesses to decide what needs to be preserved and discarded. It is also important for them to identify the limits to change, based on market evaluation, its growth rate and organization's capacity to change.

Establishing a timetable and specifying priorities has to be the next step. At this stage, it is important to have clarity about how pieces balance off one another; how changing one single element, whether a procedure, practice, policy or reward, changes the rest; how the sequence of events and its flow affect the whole structure. It would be essential to deploy the relevant know-how related to kind of activities planned for change and make it collectively available to all concerned, by way of incorporating it into the structure of the organization itself.

Effective management of change requires a system to ensure that all key actors, namely, top leadership, managers and supervisors, move in unison and fulfil particular roles based on their unique relationship to the change at hand. Top leadership must communicate directly and participate actively and visibly throughout the project. For change to be successful, managers and supervisors, who are close to action, have the responsibility that their teams must change the way they do their jobs. Employees look to their managers for answers, support and direction in times of change. They have important roles both of a communicator and an advocate of change and also that of a coach, helping employees during the transition. Only carefully planned and implemented change efforts can help organizations adapt significantly to shifting conditions and improve their competitive standing, providing a far better future.

CHAPTER 9

Vision for Change

The best way to predict the future—is to create it.
—Peter Drucker

Vision is a futuristic, concise and clear description of the goal to be achieved and the reality that we wish to create. It is a picture for people of what the organization will look like and serves to inspire commitment, motivate and engage people. Vision provides meaning and purpose to the work of the organization and encourages people to work to strive for its attainment.

According to Lucas,[17]

> The purpose of a vision is to guide (lead people in the direction of goals), to remind (what the organization wants to be), to inspire (people and their behavior), to control (organizational activities and processes in the direction of the vision), and to free employees (from tradition and a past that is irrelevant).

It also reveals the culture and values of an organization and its core competencies. An inspiring vision can help overcome the hesitation to espouse change that comes from anxiety arising from uncertainty.

There are three parts of a well-conceived vision:

1. What does the company stand for (its values)?
2. What for does the company exist? What will be missed by the society if this company was/is not existing?

3. Where does the company want to go (envisioned future) and how it will further/impact the previous two?

Kotter[18] states:

> The guiding coalition (for change) develops a picture of the future that is relatively easy to communicate and appeals to customers, stockholders, and employees. A vision always goes beyond the numbers and helps clarify the direction in which an organization needs to move. Eventually, a strategy for achieving that vision is also developed. If you can't communicate the vision to someone in five minutes or less and get a reaction that signifies both, understanding and interest, you are not yet done with this phase of transformation.

In the case studies reported earlier, we observed the group chairperson of Mega Corporation had been talking about his expectations, including a few vision-related statements but it still needed focus and clarity, to be termed as vision. The question was: Change to what? One business head shared that the group chairperson had neither any vision nor conviction but had only wishful thinking of an ideal state. He used to make statements which would look like vision but had no belief in them. He knew how to say those things and those ad hoc statements could not be taken as vision. Ultimately, it was the core group which debated and finalized the vision for change. In AG Corporation, the vision for change was finalized through a two-day workshop attended by top team and various heads of departments. The strategy to create a shared vision was worked out by the core group consisting of top executives.

While the vision is the picture of an end state where all the plans and strategies will eventually take us, the plan specifies step by step how to implement a strategy and the strategy shows how to achieve a vision. Through vision we try to see a possible future, and the well-thought-out plans and strategies make our journey on the road to change comparatively free of roadblocks. Joel Barker, a well-known author who has written extensively on vision and discovered the concept of paradigms, has mentioned that vision without action is a dream. Action without vision is simply passing time. Action with vision is making a positive difference.

It is also important that vision and strategies are logical and unambiguous. Blurred and illogical visions and strategies cannot be communicated with clarity and sound logic. With large-scale discontinuous change, where we venture into unknown territory, it is important to set the vision and strategies correctly. Bold visions would need bold strategies.

It is important that the dominant coalition (to be discussed in the next chapter) not only develops a shared vision but also disseminates it so that it becomes the shared vision of the organization, preferably by taking inputs from rest of the employees/groups. Shared vision is a source for creating a common identity and discipline, which establishes a focus on mutual purpose and changes people's relationship with the organization. People begin to work together by developing shared images of the future they wish to create. Shared vision binds people together in a common cause and creates a moral commitment to it. Developing a shared vision or commitment to vision becomes easier if people participate in planning and implementing the change programme. People always support what they help to create.

The core group in Mega Corporation considered promoting acceptance and developing support for change vision to be the most critical aspect of the strategy as it involved moving people out of their comfort zones. Accordingly, the core group members interacted with various groups of employees to develop a shared vision.

Shared sense of desirable future helps motivate and coordinate actions that create transformations. If individuals or groups become involved in the change, they tend to see it as their change, rather than one imposed upon them. We should be able to create passion amongst people to break out of routines and take ownership for change.

Even though employees embrace the new vision, they sometimes feel disempowered by certain obstacles, such as compensation or reward system, which can force them to choose between the new vision and their self-interest. We must be able to foresee and remove such obstacles.

Rakesh Balachandran introduces an interesting caveat: 'If the job of your team is to only execute a strategy pre-determined by corporate headquarters, probably a planning and execution session would do your team better than a visioning exercise.'[19] His other advices are equally pertinent:

1. We have to pay attention to the time horizon for creating a vision. He adds 'Anything too short is meaningless—anything too long will not be motivating enough for most teams.'
2. Though there are several tools for planning the visioning exercise, he recommends Lego Serious play. Of course, facilitators and business leaders should concur.
3. To make shared vision meaningful for the masses, it is also important to spell out the acceptable and unacceptable behaviours in the pursuit of shared vision.
4. It is important in the very beginning to spell what will be milestones for shared vision.

We will be talking about the need and importance of milestones in planning and implementation of change in subsequent chapters.

CHAPTER 10

Building a Dominant Coalition

Even an extremely talented and charismatic person may not have enough time, skills, energy and leadership capacity to lead change all alone, except in very small organizations. Therefore, the need for a dominant coalition is imperative. The dominant coalition is a group of members in key influencing positions who combine their resources and become more powerful than when they each act alone. It is a group formed to pursue a strategy to achieve the goal of change, knowing that their personal success is also dependent on the success of others. This team is involved in setting direction for the change, identifying options and narrowing down on resources and support from various parts of the organization. As change progresses throughout large organizations, additional teams are also formed at lower levels to help drive action within their units.

> In Mega Corporation, as we have mentioned earlier, the first step was to put together a dominant coalition between potential sources of energy that could direct the change effort.

According to Kotter,[10] there are four key characteristics for an effective coalition:

1. *Position power:* Are there enough key players on board, especially main line managers, so that those left out cannot easily block progress?

2. *Expertise:* Are the various points of view—in terms of discipline, work experience, nationality and so on—relevant to the task at hand adequately represented so that informed, intelligent decisions will be made?
3. *Credibility:* Does the group have enough people with good reputation within the firm so that its pronouncements will be taken seriously by employees?
4. *Leadership:* Does the group include enough proven leaders to be able to drive the change process?

Diversity is essential, not only of functional knowledge and parts of the organization but also of approaches.

The constitution of a task force is a key element of change management. Ignoring any of the above elements can seriously impede the success of the effort in two ways. If the key influencers have been left out, their support may become suspect due to either indifference or ego hassles due to a feeling of being left out. On the other hand, if inconsequential persons are co-opted for any reason, political or otherwise, this may dissipate the energy and focus of the coalition because comparisons of contributions may occur. Apart from the criteria as laid out by Kotter, what should be the personal qualities or commitments of the members of the dominant coalition?

Boyett and Boyett[20] have listed the following attributes of the coalition members and their duties to:

- Share a keen sense of discomfort with the way things are.
- Agree on a vision for the future.
- Have a good reputation.
- Control key resources (time, money, and people) that will be necessary for the change effort.
- Control the rewards and punishments and are willing to use them to achieve the vision.
- Demonstrate public support for the change and convey in their words and deeds a strong commitment to realizing the vision.
- Be in for the long haul.

Kotter[10] advised that people with fat egos and snakes should be kept out of the dominant coalition:

> ...people who create enough mistrust to kill teamwork. At senior levels in most organizations, people have large egos. But unless they also have a realistic sense of their weaknesses and limitations, unless they can appreciate complementary strengths in others, and unless they can subjugate their immediate interests to some greater goal, they will probably contribute about as much to a guiding coalition as does nuclear waste.

The five business heads, along with the change facilitator, formed the top transformation team (core group) in Mega Corporation. Change facilitator was the facilitator of the core group as the internal facilitator brings with him an understanding of the organizational culture and politics, and his own biases serve as a useful counterpoint to the biases of the line leaders on the team. Fortunately, all the members of the core group had, by and large, the characteristics as considered essential by Kotter, and Boyett and Boyett. They also had the non-traditional mind set and were willing to venture into unchartered territory, conditions necessary for success.

After the formation of an effective team, a visible and dynamic coalition, which was a major step in getting around the problems, the group diagnosed the situation and came up with the desired vision for change. Their two-day workshop allowed the group to examine their personal styles and dispositions, and to ensure that there were no hurdles in the free flow of energy. For the new roles and relationships, it was necessary that frequent and consistent communication take place. Now it needed a process or means to get there.

Kotter states that regardless of the process used, trust is a necessary component. When there is trust, you can create teamwork. When it is missing, you cannot.[10] Rajan recalls a similar experience. One large industrial group in Oman wanted training on trust conducted for its top team of all the group companies in 2005. Until then, he had done training on such subjects as leadership and team building, and this was a unique request. The group chairperson gave an interesting rationale: 'Leadership, teaming, etc. all depend on trust. If trust is there, everything else is there. Otherwise, there is nothing.'

It is also natural that the commitment can wither. Off-site teambuilding events can be useful to reinforce energy, understanding and mutual respect.

A well-functioning guiding team is able to articulate and put to rest questions such as: What change is needed? What is the vision of the new organization? What should not be altered? What is the best way to make the vision a reality? What change strategies are unacceptably dangerous? Good answers to these questions position an organization to leap into a promising future.

The core group members of Mega Industry's change management team, therefore, emphasized the need for a sense of partnership with each other where contributions would be respected and a real consensus would be established before committing the team to action. The core group, therefore, laid down the following ground rules for its functioning:

1. Absolute confidentiality
2. Open mind
3. Mutual trust
4. Transparency
5. Information sharing
6. Regular interaction
7. Group vision/interest

Besides these ground rules, the core group arrived at an understanding with regard to its functioning and facing the challenge of change. They included:

1. We shall meet on a regular basis to share information, review the situation and take decisions.
2. We shall start giving the right signals that we mean business with no compromises.
3. Onus of improvement and bringing change is on us; however, we need the chairperson's sponsorship.
4. In the corporate and professional world, we command great respect but have an image that we cannot manage our affairs. We shall improve our image.
5. Our approach to change, especially IR-related issues, shall:

   a. be fair, benevolent and caring. However, we shall take principled stand for developing the right work culture.
   b. try our best to bring change without confrontation; however, we shall not shy away from it if warranted.

6. We shall take charge of the situation under each one of us with the belief that it can be done and we shall do it.
7. Each one of us will try to exercise better discipline.
8. We shall work as a team, with joint responsibility for all businesses/operations of the group, holding a 'Mega Corporation' perspective.
9. All major issues pertaining to any division shall be decided jointly so that each one is aware of the background of the decision/action taken.

During the first off-site meeting of the core group, the business heads diagnosed that they had shown complete lack of ownership in managing their businesses. There was overemphasis on 'somehow' achieving production targets without giving any importance to the process or discipline. While handling various difficult situations during the change process, doubts still persisted within the core group members that the chairperson might interdict, but their consensus and firm stance prevented him from doing so. There were occasions when the chairperson did show signs of developing cold feet, but unified voice of the core group prevailed. It had turned into a dominant coalition. Despite differences, the core group members felt a sense of partnership, exercised self-restraint and a real consensus was established before committing the team to action. All the business heads felt that the best thing that happened during the change process was that core group members held together as a team, worked with trust and transparency, everybody was party to the decisions and felt bound by and to it.

Similarly, in AG Corporation, the core group of top five executives who had the required expertise, credibility and control over key resources, were committed to the vision of change and felt a sense of partnership. The core group used to meet every day to discuss strategic issues relating to change, take vital decisions and monitor the implementation of change process. This is another success story of a dominant coalition.

People emulate and draw inspiration from the conduct of their superiors. We cannot hope to create an environment for change when the top team is perceived to be a non-cohesive group of individuals pursuing individual goals at the cost of organizational goals. The success of teamwork depends largely on the capacity of the individuals to look beyond their narrow horizons of ego, self-gain and individual glory by following the path of self-restraint, self-control and selflessness.

CHAPTER 11

Designing Change Strategy

In the change process, we have to implement the plans to bring about new ways of working. This, in turn, seeks to disengage from the past and choose new attitudes and mindset. We, therefore, need to coach and build new skills and competencies to enable people to remain competitive. The change strategy should consider training of employees in new skills, competencies, ideas, approaches and behaviour.

Designing an appropriate change strategy involves setting out clearly defined vision, objectives and strategic intent. It is important to identify where we can secure early wins, creating supporting alliances, scheduling the steps that must take place throughout the change cycle and the way in which it would be brought about, with focus on details.

Prahalad[21] states the following important points while designing a strategic architecture:

1. Emotional and the intellectual energy for going through the transition.
2. A shared aspiration binds, unites and inspires everyone to stretch beyond current resources.

In the process of designing a change programme, due attention must also be paid to people's issues and concerns. The systems and processes to be used are equally important part of strategy.

Sometimes, the entire process is production and function driven and neglects the cultural change which we intend to bring. The top management team or dominant coalition, which gives a shape to the change programme and determines new organizational structure, could sometimes lack sensitivity to issues and concerns of the people.

The change strategy must also include a plan of appraising progress on a continuous basis to exercise control and acting if unexpected deviations occur. It should, however, be kept in mind that change takes time and should not be forced to occur too quickly. People need to be provided with the time and opportunity to disengage from the present state to which they are used to and feel a natural attachment. The strategy should also contain measures to deal with one of the biggest midcourse challenges to keep the change process focused and energized.

Wang[22] presents eight change management strategies that are quite effective:

1. Change managers at the top directly impact the success. Therefore, the CEO must align the best team at the top. These people must be very strong communicators.
2. They should ask for feedback even before they begin. Quite often, feedback from the lower levels is not taken and that is where maximum resistance is faced later.
3. They should share the exact statistics instead of vague homilies.
4. Keep it simple, one at a time. Things have a natural tendency to become complicated with the passage of time. Guard against that. Do not attempt too much at a time.
5. As John Beshears and Francesca Gino[23] state in an *HBR* article, create an experimental group and a control group. It means that, where possible, attempt the change as a pilot project in one part of the organization and use the result to fine tune the strategy.
6. Emotion is as much a part of change as the data. Harness emotions towards change. Wang[22] states: 'Don't overestimate the value of the dollar; don't underestimate the heartstrings.'
7. Set up small wins. Make it a point to recognize and reward people along the way, through a formal reward and recognition programme. This strengthens the constituency for change.
8. Communicate, communicate and communicate.

One of the prerequisites of an effective change programme is the establishment of credibility of the management's intentions about the proposed change. Chances of success of change programme increase considerably once the employees perceive that management has good intentions.

It is important that entry points be carefully weighed. Quite often, change facilitators or top management allow their own perceptions or biases to guide what should be the first entry point. Back in early 1980s, Rajan was working on a turnaround strategy for one of the loss-making public sector undertakings. Armed with specialized knowledge on organization design from one of the top gurus on the subject, late Dr B. L. Maheshwari, director, Centre for Organizational Development, he found that the organization had a poor structure. So a meeting was arranged between Dr Maheshwari and the managing director of the organization. Later, Dr Maheshwari remarked that the main challenge of this organization was faulty strategy and not the structure. This enlightenment was very useful in Rajan's subsequent consulting assignments. Quite often, managements would ask for training or climate survey or the type of intervention of their choice as a remedy for their problems. Without contradicting their 'wisdom', Peter Block's methodology of organization priority survey that sought to collate perceptions of senior/top management of relative priority concerns amongst strategy, inappropriate structure, negative climate, ineffective systems and processes, unbalanced power relationships, underdeveloped individuals, ineffective teamwork, unclear aims and objectives, unassertive leadership and so on in a forced choice format. The collated data were fed back to the top management, which they did not deny because the inputs came from them. This would immediately help build consensus on the agenda ahead and was productively used across countries with suitable modifications.

Of course, alternative methodologies exist, but shared priorities of the top management are critical for the unity of purpose and approach.

12

Handling Resistance

We should paralyze resistance with persistence.
—Woody Hayes, famous
American football coach

Why We Resist Change

Routines represent our zones of comfort, and we do not want to come out of them, as there is a sense of predictability about them. These routines have structured our thoughts in a certain way. Comfort with the status quo is extremely powerful, and fear of moving into an unknown future state creates anxiety and insecurity. Negativity or lack of enthusiasm is, thus, a normal human response to change. We should, therefore, never be surprised by it, rather should expect resistance and work with patience, giving time to people to undergo the psychological transition which takes place during the process of change. We are dealing with emotions of people while trying to change their mental models and mindset, and this has to be done with lot of persistence, tact and sensitivity.

Kotter and Schlesinger[24] cited four most common reasons for employees' resistance to change:

- *Parochial self-interest:* People often resist change because they think they might lose something of value as a result of that change.
- *Misunderstanding and lack of trust:* People are often not very clear about the implications of change. Misunderstanding is highly likely if there is lack of trust between employees and the management.
- *Different assessments:* Frequently employees assess the situation differently from their managers. They might see more costs rather than benefits resulting from change.
- *Low tolerance for change:* Sometimes people resist change because they are unsure if they acquire the new skills and abilities that the change requires.

Professor Matti Otala views resistance to change as fully natural and human and says that there are many sources of resistance:

- The comfort of old habits
- Selectivity of attention and retention
- Dependence on role model's example
- Fear of the unknown
- Economics
- Lack of trust
- Misunderstanding
- Parochial self-interest
- Different assessments of what change is needed
- Low tolerance for change (attitude)[25]

On the aspect of why individuals resist change, Hari Gopal[26] brings in the concept of divergence from their mental models:

Changing the mental map causes discomfort or pain. The discomfort is less if the discrepancy/dissonance between this mental map and the change activity is minimal. The greater the dissonance, the greater the discomfort and higher resistance allowing for fewer changes in one's behavior. If the discrepancy is very high, individuals tend to reduce the dissonance by either disregarding the external reality or modifying their own 'mental map'.[26]

Presented next is an exercise based on Jeffrey Russell and Linda Russell's illustrative list[27] of the perceived losses of change and we invite readers to draft their responses in each case.

What the employees may fear	*What you will plan, do or say to address these fears? How will you turn this into an opportunity?*
1. *Job security:* People may fear job loss or a loss of financial resources due to a reduction in their job or income level.	
2. *Psychological comfort or security:* People may feel that the change threatens their level of safety, comfort, security and self-confidence by reducing their level of certainty about the world around them.	
3. *Control over one's future:* People may perceive that the change threatens their ability to control their future actions, decisions and identity.	
4. *Purpose or meaning:* People may believe that change threatens to take away the identities, hopes and aspirations that make their lives meaningful.	

(Contd.)

(Contd.)

What the employees may fear	What you will plan, do or say to address these fears? How will you turn this into an opportunity?
5. *Competence:* People may feel unprepared for new responsibilities and duties, which can lead to embarrassment and a reduction in self-confidence.	
6. *Social connections:* People may believe that their social contacts with customers, co-workers or managers will disappear. This can result in a loss in their sense of belonging to a team, group or the organization. Since so much of our sense of self evolves through our relationships to others, this tends to be the most traumatic.	
7. *Territory:* People believe they may lose a sense of certainty about the territory or area that used to be theirs. This territory includes physical workspace, expertise, job titles, assignments and psychological space.	
8. *Future opportunities:* People may fear that they may lose a deserved reward that they have worked hard to achieve.	

What the employees may fear	*What you will plan, do or say to address these fears? How will you turn this into an opportunity?*
9. *Power:* Change can threaten a person's sense of power and influence in their organization and life. People may perceive that the change takes away part of what enables them to feel effective.	
10. *Social status:* People may perceive that the change will erode their status that they have achieved (through competence, influence or hard work) compared to other people. They fear that what they have worked hard to accomplish may disappear.	
11. *Trust in others:* People may lose their trust and faith in others—especially leaders and others whom they have admired in the past—when the impending change threatens to take away other things of value.	
12. *Independence and autonomy:* People may feel that their ability to be self-directed and self-managed will be eroded.	

Environment Matters for Change

The environment or context within which the change is taking place is also important. These also need to be accounted for and strategies evolved to deal with the following:

1. Employees will keep in mind the organization's past record of changes, including reinforcements or rewards. Similarly, if the company has a history of initiating changes and not following through or allowing some groups to opt out of change, then these past events will heavily influence the willingness of employees to engage in new changes.
2. Resistance to change is normally more intense for changes that are implemented without employees' involvement and participation. In such a situation, motivation, energy level and enthusiasm of the employees decrease. There is little or very negligible scope of resistance if the impacted people are involved in planning and execution of changes that are to impact them. In the words of Peter Senge, 'People don't resist change. They resist being changed.'
3. In the present era, employees may also fear that if they agree to one change, the company may embark upon further changes, which may be more difficult to accept.
4. Friends, family, neighbours, influential persons such as union leaders, political leaders may be discouraging the employees from accepting change.
5. Sets of data and perceptions of the management and the rest of the employees may be different, and therefore they may genuinely feel that the changes may be damaging to the company/employees in the long run. On the other hand, in cases such as acquisitions, mergers, amalgamations and so on, employees' perceptions may well be true.
6. Employees may perceive a change as running counter to organizational values or their personal values. It has to be stressed from the beginning that the proposed change is in consonance with its long-held values. Alternatively, if some of the values have to be jettisoned for long-term survival and progress, the rationale

has to be properly communicated, possibly through town-hall or other large-scale interactive processes coupled with extensive communication.

People need time to work through the change process. Individuals have their own inner lives, populated by their values, beliefs, fears and aspirations. The choices they make are linked to these elements and are the extensions of reality that operates in their hearts and minds. None of us move through change at the same pace or in the same way, nor are we motivated by the same thing. One way of looking at resistance could be that we take it as feedback and use it productively. It may be useful to address resistance by individuals at the individual level through a personal conversation between the resistant employee and his superior, keeping in mind the inner dynamics that drives his thought process. This might lead us to the final tip for managing resistance.

Things to Keep in Mind While Initiating Change Process

Overcoming resistance is a process of touching what people think and feel and can be dealt with only through validation of facts and clarification about notions. If we could influence the thinking of people, feelings would automatically get influenced, as feelings are primarily the outcome of thinking. The way we communicate the change to the people has the single most important impact on how much resistance to change will occur.

When the change project is being initiated, we should be proactive about the source of potential resistance and the likely objections behind this resistance. We should act on this knowledge ahead of time before the resistance impacts the change process. To be effective at managing resistance, we must look deeper into what is ultimately causing resistance instead of looking at it from the narrow prism of a problem employee/s or problem section or area. We must identify the root causes instead of just focusing on symptoms.

Many managers underestimate the ways they can positively influence specific individuals and groups during a change. According to Kotter and Schlesinger,[24] there could be six approaches for dealing with resistance to change:

1. *Education and communication:* Useful when one needs resistors' support and resistance is based on inadequate or inaccurate information and analysis. It is time-consuming and requires efforts.
2. *Participation and involvement:* In general, this leads to commitment, not merely compliance.
3. *Facilitation and support:* This is most helpful when fear and anxiety drive resistance. It includes training. This can be time-consuming, expensive and yet fail.
4. *Negotiation and agreement:* This is particularly appropriate if some people with power to resist are likely to lose out due to change. However, this may create situations for blackmail.
5. *Manipulation and co-optation:* Management can co-opt significant potential resistors in design and/or implementation. However, this may limit the scope of education/communication and participation. Nevertheless, it is sometimes used effectively.
6. *Explicit and implicit coercion:* People can be transferred or sacked. This can lead to snowballing however.

As per the 2009 benchmark study of Prosci, the main reason for resisting change by employees was 'a lack of awareness of why the change was being made'. No one made a compelling case for why the change was being proposed, leaving employees wondering— why? Similarly, for managers the principal reason for resistance was a lack of awareness about and involvement in the change. Managers' inputs were not solicited, resulting into resistance to change.

Real power comes not from forcing people to do what we want but from changing the way people think so that they willingly do what we want. We should create a facilitating climate where behaviour is guided by genuineness, acceptance, caring, positive regard and empathy. We should listen to and allow the resisting person to express his ideas and feelings with regard to change. Hearing the employees out and letting them express their point of view in a non-judgemental environment will reduce resistance.

In Mega Corporation, during the change process itself, one of the business heads (member of the core group) continued to pursue the appeasement policy keeping the short-term business interests in mind. Under pressure from the union, he agreed to issue goggles/glares to certain category of workers and granted two increments to the workers of the assembly department for shifting to new assembly line, erected very close to the old assembly line, though it did not involve any additional workload. Not only were these unjustified concessions granted to the union in a closed-door meeting with the divisional representatives of the union, a commitment was also taken from them that this should be kept a top secret and no one else outside the division, especially the change facilitator, should know about it. When the change facilitator, during one-to-one discussions with the said business head, wanted to verify the factual position, he denied having taken any such decision.

Since it was not only a question of serious repercussions of the decisions on other business divisions but of basic integrity, attitude and commitment of a member of the core group to the vision of change, and also involved the underlying ethics and principles of running business, the change facilitator sought the intervention of group chairman. In his note to chairman, with the details of two incidents, he wrote:

> With profound anguish and regret, I wish to bring to your kind attention a few incidents related to X division, which involve deeper dilemma and malaise relating to:
>
> 1. Independence of a company in functional matters even when it has deeper repercussions on the functioning of the other companies in the entire Mega group.
> 2. Common vision and commitment to cultural transformation.

3. Short-sighted appeasement policies, undermining ethics and imperatives of shared goals.

These incidents highlight appeasement, abject surrender before negative elements, deliberate concealment of information, and willful disregard of corporate concerns. Needless to say, they are turning the clock back on our common task of bringing about change in work culture and have led to cascading problems everywhere else. I am forced to seek your intervention to settle the issue once and for all.

The chairperson discussed the issue with the business head; post which the change facilitator focused on developing greater conviction and commitment for change in the concerned business head. Sometimes, managers intellectually understand the need for change but are unable to change their attitudes and behaviour. *When we change what we believe, we change what we do.* Realizing that the concerned business head was unable to make the emotional transition, the change facilitator held discussions with him, challenging his unviable beliefs and suggesting more viable and contextually relevant beliefs. Later on, the said business head proved to be the most active partner in the whole change process.

Creating Conducive Climate

One of the essential conditions for effectively handling resistance is to create a climate for change in the organization, which requires willingness and ability of the top management to change their behaviour and act as a role model. If they persist with old, dysfunctional behaviour, the rest of the organization would follow suit and pay only lip service to the change process.

It is necessary that resistance and obstacles to change be dealt with quickly and firmly. Failure to do so would lead others to lose commitment and interest in the change.

In one of the business divisions of Mega Corporation, when there was work stoppage for 20 days on the issue of transfer of a few workers to other section, the management had spoken to all concerned union leaders and the workers of the division, who did not find any mala fide intentions on the part of the management in the transfer and even accepted the logic behind the transfer but did not agree to management's right to transfer. They resisted because they were afraid of change, which could have given necessary flexibility to management to manage as per business and environmental needs. People are capable of logically and rationally considering and screening relevant facts and beliefs but their values perform a gatekeeping function. Values represent what we consider to be important in life and act as criteria for making decisions. These people wanted to remain the same without anybody disturbing their comfort levels, which was important for them. Reassuring those who are afraid of change by using consoling words may often in itself prevent the process of change and the management, therefore, taking a firm stand, started taking disciplinary action against those involved in instigating the unjustified work stoppage. The workers finally came up with the offer of restoring normalcy provided they were paid wages for the period of work stoppage, as has been the practice in the past, in all business divisions. Besides the fact that the demand was wholly unjustified, the management did not want to give any wrong signal by way of extending any concession, and thus, did not accept any condition for restoring normalcy. Normal working was finally resumed after 20 days. Managers had a belief that things were difficult to change, as the management cannot take a firm stand. The stand taken by the management in the said case not only activated managers but also encouraged the fence sitters to join actively in the change process.

Similarly, when the workers once agitated over the settlement-related issues of production norms and new work practices, the casual workers and overtime were stopped by the union. The management took a firm stand to demonstrate its resolve that it was committed to change. Though only casual workers and overtime were stopped, but there was no production at all and hence the regular workers were also not paid any wage, on the principle of no work no wage. The union, in view of past experiences, had not expected such a tough stand by the management. Finally, the union started approaching the management, requesting for some face-saving device, so that the agitation could be called off, but the management firmly refused to extend any concession and the agitation was finally called off unconditionally.

The firm stand of the management in the agitation of 20 days over the issue of transfer and the one-month-long current agitation gave it confidence and established its seriousness about the change. The whole management was highly motivated and pursued the change process with confidence. They believed that change was possible and took charge of the situation in their respective areas. When the driving forces outweigh the restraining forces, it becomes easier to affect the change. Managers, with higher level of confidence, started exercising control, resulting into improved discipline and weakening of restraining forces.

Morris and Raben[28] talk about the first question in the minds of employees as WIIFM (What is in it for me or what is going to happen to me). 'The task of management will be to somehow relieve that anxiety and motivate constructive behavior.'

A good portion of the normal resistance disappears when employees are clear about the benefits the change will bring to them as individuals. Nothing is more important to individual employees than to know the positive impact on their own lives and career. Readiness to change will tend to be greater if we can convince people that there could always be a new and better situation.

With the change in environment, after the one-month-long agitation was called off in Mega Corporation, and the management was, to a great extent, in control of the situation, anxiety levels went up and people started fearing as to what was going to happen to them. This was time to give emotional support to people by way of information, support and counselling about the change. An effort was, therefore, made by all the managers to define new terms and persuade employees to accept them. Another goal of such one-to-one discussion was to help people feel engaged and committed to the organization's future and satisfy their need to feel respected, understood, listened to and valued along the way.

It was observed that during one-to-one discussions all these workers and the union leaders would agree verbally; however, they failed to follow through. Lack of trust emerged as a serious barrier. If people have trouble trusting each other during routine times, they trust each other even less during times of change.

One of the paradoxes of change is that trust is hardest to establish when we need it the most. Mistrust causes people to focus on protecting themselves instead of cooperating with change efforts.

The last strike engineered by the negative leadership was the final test for the management to demonstrate its commitment for change and that there could be no compromise on basic issues, linked to the survival of the group. The time to nurse the change resistors or to convince them about the inevitability of change was over. It was the time to lay down the law and tell everyone clearly that the game had changed and that they could either play within the new rules or play somewhere else. The government declared the strike to be illegal and all those involved in instigating and inciting workers and other acts of indiscipline, including a few leaders of the union, were dismissed. The message was loud and clear and had the desired impact. The strike was called off unconditionally and negotiations resumed to finalize the settlement.

It is not science that you can lay down a formula for dealing with resistance. As long as humans are involved, every situation will be similar and yet unique. There will be several options, and one will have to choose the most appropriate option using experience and wisdom.

One can minimize resistance through proactive dialogue, establishing shared meanings and interpretations and donning the role of a coach and facilitator instead of regulator, commander and a bureaucrat.

Change initiative may start with great enthusiasm and total involvement of top management but, many a time, the effort gets bogged down during implementation either due to day-to-day issues or in view of some short-term objective. The emphasis on day-to-day issues and priorities or the short-term profits during the process of change has the potential of ruining the change programme. The organization must be careful enough not to risk the change programme for such short-term gains. They have the potential not only of ruining the change programme but also of management losing its credibility. Any organization undergoing the process of change must also not fall in the trap of holding on to its old ways of doing things. In the words of Peter Drucker, 'The greatest danger in times of turbulence is not the turbulence—it is to act with yesterday's logic.'

**Key Points to Know about the Employees'
Resistance to Change**

1. Resistance happens for a reason or some reasons. They have to be addressed.
2. Plan for and expect resistance. Begin dialogue even before commencing change to reduce surprise and resistance.
3. Be patient and allow employees to work it out within their system while offering support.
4. There could be a very important lesson or a warning for the organization in employee resistance.

CHAPTER 13

Sustaining Change

Sustaining change means sticking with initiatives, making sure that desired changes happen and outcomes are delivered. For any change to be sustained, it needs to seep into the bloodstream of the corporate body and become embedded in the organization's culture. Until new behaviour is rooted in social norms and shared values, changes are subject to degradation as soon as change pressures start diminishing.

Steps to Cultural Change

A culture truly changes only when a new way of operating has been shown to succeed over a stipulated period of time. Real change does not take hold until people actually change what they do. Trying to shift the norms and values before we have created the new way of operating does not work. We can create new behaviours that reflect a desired culture, but those new behaviours will not become norms until the very end of the process.

In this last phase of change, we keep it in place by helping to create a new, supportive and sufficiently strong organizational culture by integrating the changed behaviour and attitude into the normal way of doing things. A supportive culture provides roots for the new ways of operating. The change leaders help employees integrate the changed behaviour or attitude into the normal way of doing things, making change stick by nurturing a new culture, new group norms of behaviour and shared values. Once it is an integral part of the culture, the new behaviour stands strongly rooted even if the leadership changes.

Culture is a complex concept. To ensure that the new norms of behaviour and skills become part of the new culture, it is important to make sure that changes last by implementing sustainable discipline in the organization. Employees need help maintaining new behaviours, especially when their old ways of working are deeply ingrained and there could be strong possibilities of their backsliding into dysfunctional habitual patterns of old behaviour. Leaders must focus on key behaviours having high impact on important issues and must take personal responsibility for ensuring that they do what they say. Leaders must also provide opportunities for employees to practice desired behaviours repeatedly and should personally model new ways of working. It is also important that management processes and systems such as promotions, succession planning, training and appraisal procedures, rewards, organizational design and policies are refined and aligned to support change. Change leaders must create an appropriate architecture of roles, responsibilities, systems and overall context that facilitates effective execution.

Once employees exhibit the new behaviours or attitudes, it is important to give positive reinforcement, establish systems to support these new behaviours and attitudes including rewards for new behaviour, and sanctions for the old. This is also the time when change leaders should focus on continuous development of employees through training and education, provide additional coaching and modelling to reinforce the stability of change and establish systems that support and encourage the new behaviours and attitudes.

When changes are taking shape and people have embraced new ways of working, the organization is ready to refreeze, which helps people and the organization to institutionalize the changes. Once the changes are institutionalized and become part of the new culture, it is ensured that the changes become the new way of functioning. With this new-found stability, every employee also finds comfort and confidence.

The rationale for creating a new sense of stability in our everyday changing world is often questioned. Even though change may be constant in many organizations, this refreezing stage is important. Without it, employees get caught in a trap where they are not sure how things should be done. So nothing ever gets done to full capacity. In the absence of a new frozen state, it is very difficult to tackle the next change initiatives effectively.

As and when we decide to introduce any new change, it would be difficult convincing people that something needs changing if we have not allowed the most recent changes to sink in. The changes that have been brought about and have benefited the organization and the individuals will be a source of motivation to implement new changes, once institutionalized. There has to be a conscious attempt to show people how the new approaches, behaviours and attitudes have helped improve performance, and sufficient time must be taken to make sure that the next generation of the top management really does personify the new approach. We must articulate the connections between the new behaviours and corporate success.

A fragile culture can be institutionalized through promotion, a career advancement process. Promoting people who truly reflect the new culture helps in strengthening the new norms and behaviours. By putting people who have absorbed a new culture into positions of power, we create an increasingly solid and stable foundation. In turn, these representatives of the new way feel more empowered and motivated to continually deliver their best.

As part of the refreezing process, make sure that we celebrate the success of the change and thank them for enduring a painful time—this helps people to find closure, strengthens their belief in change and keeps them willing for changing future scenarios as well. Just as in most cultures around the world, people believe that the spirit may not find peace (some even believe that the spirit may even come back) if last rites are not properly performed. It is important to provide closure by removing remnants of the previous systems, processes and so on that are no longer in consonance with the new requirements.

In fact, even in cases like online ERP implementation, many a time, failure is brought about by people continuing to find comfort in off-line spreadsheets. It is important to set up a mechanism to monitor that people do not resort to old ways, or find a via media through human ingenuity, at least for six months.

Project Management Approach

Based on change efforts in more than 200 companies, Sirkin, Keenan and Jackson[29] formulated four factors that determine the outcome of any change/transformation initiative, and what they called the hard side of change management.

D. The duration of time, until the change programme is completed if it is a short lifespan, else the amount of time between reviews of milestones.

I. The project team's performance integrity; that is, its ability to complete the initiative on time. This depends on members' skills and traits relative to the project's requirements.

C. The commitment to change that top management (C_1) and employees affected by the change (C_2) display.

E. The effort over and above the usual work that the change initiative demands of the employees.

Using the study, the authors found that complex projects should be reviewed fortnightly; straightforward initiatives can be reviewed every six to eight weeks. Further, since the success of change programmes depends on the quality of teams, companies must free up the best staff, while making sure that day-to-day operations do not suffer. Members' roles, commitment and accountability are clarified, team composition and team leader's selection is carefully done based on problem-solving skills, result orientation, ambiguity tolerance, organizational savvy, willingness to accept responsibility for decisions and lack of craving for limelight.

No amount of top-level support is adequate. Writers developed a rule of thumb: When the top leaders feel that they are talking up a change initiative at least three times more than they need to, managers feel that the top leaders are backing the transformation.

Support of mid-level managers, supervisors and workers is also critical.

Project teams must calculate how much extra workload will come to employees during the change effort, in addition to their regular day-to-day work. The additional workload should not be more than 10 per cent. If it is more than 10 per cent, people shirk additional responsibility; current performance starts suffering and this, in turn, can lead to people raising doubts on the desirability of change itself.

These operational issues run the risk of being neglected. Just as no change can be brought about by neglecting the human–emotional aspects, change can also fail if the project management issues are not fully planned and taken care of.

PART IV

YOUR TOOLKIT FOR CHANGE

CHAPTER 14

It's a Team Game

Talent wins games, but teamwork and intelligence wins championship.
—Michael Jordan

Teamwork is the backbone of any successful enterprise. Pockets of individual excellence cannot solve present-day complex problems. Organizations must learn how to derive maximum benefit from the collective wisdom and generate synergy. Hellen Keller, a well-known American author, says, 'Alone we can do so little; together we can do so much.'

The commitment in exceptional teams is so high that the team members are committed to group goals above and beyond their personal goals. They see themselves as belonging to a team rather than as individuals who operate autonomously.

For effective functioning of any team, it is necessary that the team members support each other, have faith in each other and generally behave in a consistent and predictably acceptable fashion. The key note of team building and its functioning lies not in surface level skills but in basic values supplemented by obligation orientation.

Arun Wakhlu,[30] in his book *Managing from the Heart*, lists the following characteristics of good teams as follows:

1. A good team is clear about what it wants to achieve. The values associated with the vision are clearly shaped by

the members of the team. There is shared strength of a common purpose, common struggles and the enabling vision creates a focused energy towards their purpose.

2. There is strong partnership in the team and members show support for each other. There is high level of openness and trust. The mutual understanding, love and respect that is shared in a good team creates an emotional support group, which helps the team to persevere in the face of challenges.

3. Roles are clearly defined and all members know how their work fits in with the big picture. The experience, talents, knowledge, skills, contacts, spiritual and emotional strengths of all members combine and synergize into something far beyond the individual capabilities.

4. Both collaboration and harmonizing differences are used to get the best results. Differences are seen as opportunities for creative thinking and growth. Issues are always confronted and dealt with openly.

5. There are sound and understood procedures in the team as also a set of agreed norms that people have mutually worked out and follow. A common working approach is defined.

6. Relationships with other groups and teams are sound. The team is well integrated with its environment.

7. The prevailing spirit in the team is strongly 'can do' and the commitment to team goals is high. It has a powerful bias for inspired action.

8. Individual and team development needs are regularly looked at and planned for.

9. The team has a high standard of leadership and it is in the most appropriate hands.

10. The team regularly reviews its progress on the task against agreed performance standards and how it is functioning as a team. Regular reflection on experiences and conscious learning is a way of life.

11. In high-performing teams, people hold themselves mutually accountable for results. There is an atmosphere of joy and fun along with focus on the work at hand.

12. Finally, a good team is held together by spirit. It is the central dominion of the heart, in the individual and collective life of the team, which gives it the magical quality of a high-performing team.

The closer the members of a team are to their own real self, the closer they come to each other. A wholesome team, because of its common spirit, is more like an organism rather than a hierarchical structure. Everyone's thoughts, words and actions resonate with the same core. Boundaries melt away, and one's identity merges with that of the team. Each one's problem becomes everyone's problem. Everyone's strengths and resources are shared by all. Phil Jackson, American professional basketball executive and former coach, has said, 'The strength of the team is each individual member and the strength of each member is the team.'

One of the critical indicators of a learning team is that there are visible idea conflicts. Peter Senge states:

In great teams, conflict becomes productive. Even when people share a common vision, they may have different ideas about how to achieve that vision. The free flow of conflicting ideas is critical for creative thinking, for discovering new solutions no one individual would have come to on his own.[31]

The core group at Mega Corporation had its share of conflict situations and the team was not characterized by an absence of conflict. Teams normally converse through dialogue and discussion. Dialogue is the process of presenting different views to discover a new idea for a richer grasp of issues and does not seek agreement. Discussions take place with a view to take decision so as to converge on a course of action. Here, the views are presented and defended. Sometimes, the process of defending the views strongly and taking a stand about it creates a situation of conflict. Since the core group at Mega Corporation was committed to the objective of change and had faith in each other, the conflicts could be resolved keeping aside individual identity and ego.

Even with the right team in place, it takes time for the team members to align themselves in a clear direction. With clarity on objective to be achieved, as a team, the members must thoroughly understand and follow the procedures as also the set of norms that have been mutually worked out for effective functioning of the team.

Partnerships are necessary for fostering good teamwork and realizing a common purpose. Partnerships call for immense trust, and, therefore, are as much a reflection of the state of mind as they are of the physical assets of each of the contributing partners. The outcome is one real partnership with sharing and concern as its core values and which enables not only the survival but also sustaining a competitive advantage.

Key factors in team development are commitment, trust, purpose, communication, involvement and process orientation. Team members must see themselves as belonging to a team rather than as individuals who operate autonomously and should be committed to group goals. Team members must have faith in each other, support each other and feel a sense of ownership. Everyone in the team has a role, and the team understands how it fits into the overall business of the organization. Despite differences, team members must feel a sense of partnership with each other. Teamwork is the ability to work together towards a common vision. Once a team understands why it is together and where it is going, it must have a process or means to get there. The process should include problem-solving tools, regular meetings, meeting agendas and minutes, and accepted ways of dealing with problems.

The success of teamwork depends largely on the capacity of the individuals to look beyond their narrow horizons of esteem, preferences and gain, by following the path of self-restraint, self-control and renunciation. If a team is to reach its potential, each team member must be willing to subjugate his personal goals for this higher purpose.

The key to team building lies in basic values, amplified by obligation orientation. Teams break up or become weak because the leaders adhere to surface-level skills in preference to deeper values of management ethics, and there is a sense of 'entitlement and rights'.

Communication Is the Lubricant

The success of any change programme depends on persuading employees to change the way they work, which people accept only if they can be influenced to think differently about their jobs. Communication is, thus, the most essential ingredient in managing change. Studies have shown that the most common cause of failure of major change projects has been the lack of communication with those affected by the project. It is the most important tool in obtaining buy-in from employees at all levels for the changes that will be necessary to implement change project. Any organization that thinks about change but does not communicate its intention to its employees is either creating much more difficulties than necessary for itself or is heading for outright failure of the change project. Maintaining secrecy about the change programme could create mistrust, anger and resentment, all of which can destroy the programme. Kotter[10] states:

> Major change is usually impossible unless most employees are willing to help, often to the point of making short-term sacrifices. But people will not make sacrifices, even if they are unhappy with the status quo, unless they think the potential benefits of change are attractive and unless they really believe that a transformation is possible. Without credible communication, and a lot of it, employee's hearts and minds are never captured.

Employees need information and guidance on why the change is necessary and the effect it will have on them. Communication can help in overcoming their sense of insecurity, which they naturally feel as their comfort zones and methods begin to shake up. It is reassuring for them to have their fear acknowledged. Organizations, therefore, need to communicate to employees what the change is, how it will occur and why the change was necessary. Paint a threadbare image of current state and a vision of a new state using success stories to boost their confidence. Employees should feel assured that changes will make things better. If we operate in secrecy or under-communicate, people would fill communication voids with rumours, attributing the worst possible motives to those in control. Dave Ulrich states:

> Companies have no choice but to try to engage not only the body but also the mind and soul of every employee. Employee contributions go up when employees feel free to share ideas, when they feel that key individuals in the firm have their interests in mind, and when they feel a valid and valued employment relationship with the firm.[32]

The following things are important in communication:

1. Drawing etymological connection with another word, communion, John Maxwell says that communication is not transmission of knowledge of ideas, but to 'connect' with the other. How can we present it as a 'heart-to-heart' talk?
2. Even at the risk of repetition to the extent of being boring, do it again and again.
3. Trying to create a consensus. Jack Welch states, 'Consistency, simplicity, and repetition is what it's all about.... It requires countless hours of eyeball-to-eyeball back and forth. It involves more listening than talking. It is a constant, interactive process aimed at (creating) consensus.'[14]

In a recent edition of the *Fortune* magazine, Jack Welch is further quoted as saying:

> You have got to talk about change every second of the day. When you say something, say it with well-chosen words, say it with your eyes, say it with your body. Then say it with your head and heart. Then say it again. And again. Till you get the feel that you have been understood.[33]

The essence of a situation is sometimes hard to express, so the leaders must make use of different modes such as images, symbols, stories and allegorical language. We need to show people something that addresses their anxieties and evokes faith in the vision. In today's high-tech age, we can develop a dramatic situation through presentations, using evidence we can see not just words and numbers. This might get people grounded in different contexts and with different experiences to grasp things intuitively, and move out of bunkers, ready to move ahead with a sense of urgency. We must, however, remember that *all communication should be honest, even if it is unpleasant. Honesty further reinforces clean intent.*

Alignment of managerial group being a critical success factor, communicating a clear image of the future to them is the first step for managing change. This managerial group, consisting of middle and line managers, is the one which comes in direct contact with the employees and can play a significant role in developing awareness of the changing business environment and also support for change.

Kotter lists seven keys to communicating effectively[10]:

I. Simplicity: Effective communication is directly related to the clarity and simplicity of the message. Focused, jargon-free information can be disseminated to large groups of people at a fraction of the cost of clumsy, complicated communication. Techno-babble and MBA-speak just get in the way, creating confusion, suspicion and alienation. Communication seems to work best when it is so direct and so simple that it has a sort of elegance.

II. Metaphors, analogies, examples: Colorful language has great power to communicate complicated ideas quickly and effectively. Well-chosen words can make a message memorable, even if it has to compete with hundreds of other communications for people's attention.

III. Multiple forums: Communication is most effective when many different vehicles are used—large group meetings, memos, newspapers, posters, and informal one-on-one talks. When the same message comes from six different directions, it stands a better chance of being heard and remembered.

IV. Repetition: The most carefully crafted messages rarely sink deep into the recipient's consciousness after only one pronouncement. Our minds are too cluttered, and any communication has to fight hundreds of other ideas for attention. All successful cases of major change seem to include tens of thousands of communications that help employees to grapple with difficult intellectual and emotional issues.

V.   Leadership by example: Often the most powerful way to communicate a new direction is through behavior. When the top five or fifty people all live the change vision, employees will usually grasp it better than if there had been a hundred stories in the in-house newsletter. When they see top management acting out the vision, a whole set troublesome questions about credibility and game playing tends to evaporate.

VI.   Explanation of seeming inconsistencies: In successful transformations, important inconsistencies in the message employees are getting are almost addressed explicitly. If mixed signals can't be eliminated, they are usually explained, simply and honestly.

VII.   Give and take: Communication is often such a difficult activity that it can easily turn into a screeching, one-way broadcast in which useful feedback is ignored and employees are inadvertently made to feel unimportant. In highly successful change efforts, this rarely happens, because communication always becomes a two-way endeavor. Even more fundamentally, two-way discussions are an essential method of helping people answer all the questions that occur to them in a transformation effort.

J. D. Duck, focusing on the need for repeated communication says that unless managers have talked enough number of times for people to start believing, interpret and internalize in their mindset, the communication is inadequate.[34]

Just disseminating information so many times, however, is not enough. James A. Champy, while stressing upon the need of two-way communication, says that instead of communication, what we need is conversation. Not only these conversations should be across the organization, they should be about the drivers and implications of the whole effort.[35]

The focus of communication strategy in Mega Corporation and AG Corporation was to communicate continuously and tirelessly in all directions, to every member of the organization, regardless of position or seniority. The situation in the company was analysed; purpose of communication was established for different target groups, keeping in mind their interests and approach to change; and clear objectives were laid down before creating messages and selecting the mediums. Since inadequate communication is one of the chief reasons cited for failed change efforts, all out efforts were made to create relevant and meaningful messages for different target groups to maximize impact. There were three main target groups for communication and the messages were clearly and appropriately created for them every time, depending on the context and the content of communication. Besides regular meetings with managers and the union, circulars were sent frequently, addressed to workers, supervisors and managers, to keep all concerned informed of the developments and sharing facts, progression in thought and information. The union was a totally divided house, with major differences and divergence of opinions based on the personal agenda of leaders, and this was proving to be a major obstacle in implementing the change program. It was therefore considered desirable to communicate directly with the workers. Since an honest and direct mention of this fact in the circulars to workers could have offended the union, thereby further complicating the situation, disguised circulars were issued, which were seemingly addressed to managers and supervisors, but meant for and made accessible to the workforce. In these circulars, the dissensions within the union, proving to be main obstacle for the settlement, were highlighted so that the workers could exercise pressure on leadership for an early and just settlement.

Managers of all the business divisions were communicated the vision for change, a clear image of the future state and its process. This was done by all the business heads and the change facilitator (members of core group) jointly. This was two-way, face-to-face communication, where they were encouraged to challenge, question, seek clarifications and come out with disagreements and apprehensions. We should remember that employees' views, concerns and questions are important and constructive, not threats. Communication meetings took place in various business divisions, which were marked by active participation and evoked interest and commitment. These communication meetings were of great help in motivating the managers and giving them the confidence that the management was supporting them wholeheartedly.

Similarly, presentations made by business heads before the executive body of the union were also a part of the communication strategy. This was also two-way, face-to-face communication where the union was communicated the picture of existing business scenario vis-à-vis competition, present position of the company and future business plans. Hard comparative data of the company and those of competitors were made available, and a compelling picture was created of the opportunities available and also of the risks of not changing. The union president later mentioned that the best part of the management's strategy was the presentation made by business heads to the union. It was a great attempt at creating comprehensive awareness.

In a situation where we intend sharing a holistic perspective of what needs to be done, top-down communication might become necessary but cannot be fully realized without a horizontal channel as well. Change cannot be enforced from the top level down but needs to be understood and adapted by all involved so that the resistance against change is minimized.

Besides the clarity and simplicity of the message, it is also important to be aware of the psychology of the target group and the communication should be customized, also keeping in mind the timings and the occasion. We must strike the right notes of optimism and realism and carefully calibrate the timing, tone, contents and positioning of every message. We can communicate more effectively when we know what pieces of information people need to know at a particular time and what the feelings of the persons involved are. Arguments would fail to convince people unless we relate to the audience at the right emotional level. With focused and tailored approach, we should be able to walk into the shoes of another, in the right way and at the right time to generate the desired response. When we truly know how the other person feels, we can communicate with him more easily and lead more effectively.

Even efficient managers either under-communicate or inadvertently send inconsistent messages. In 1993, Wyatt Company (now Watson Wyatt Worldwide) investigated 531 US organizations undergoing major restructuring. Wyatt asked the CEOs, 'if you could go back and change one thing, what would it be?' The most frequent answer: 'The way I communicated with my employees.' An effective communication plan is one that contains the four critical elements of communication, namely the right message, to the right audience, at the right time and from preferred senders.

The right attitude and honest intentions in communicating with our employees can help us take a giant leap towards winning employee trust and commitment. True commitment is the energy or enthusiasm that drives every employee, irrespective of the level at which he is working. If we are honest and our expression is true to our experience, our communication becomes authentic. As a wise Indian sage put it: 'May my word be firmly established in my mind. May my mind be firmly established in my word.'

Authenticity and credibility in communication is possible only through consistency in conduct. People trust others when there is transparency of action, when they are told that something will be initiated or completed, and it does. Ineffective communication, especially during the period of change, results in either creating or increasing mistrust and that is why there is a need for effective and persuasive communication, especially during periods of major change.

In AG Corporation, communication played a vital role in creating awareness, promoting acceptance and developing support for change. Being a small unit, the focus was on two-way face-to-face communication meetings with managers and supervisors, sharing need, plan and strategies. The approach was to communicate continuously and tirelessly. Understanding the importance of communication and preparing the organization for change, the CEO himself was conducting all communication meetings, and it had the desired impact. It was through these meetings that a shared vision was created, and all the employees got involved in the process of change.

Role of the Front-Line Supervisors

Prosci's research says that when a supervisor tells an employee about a major restructuring project, she may include the business reasons for change, the risk of not changing, and the urgency to remain competitive, he and his family hear that the company is in trouble and he may not have a job post-change.

The supervisor needs to talk to the employee about how the change will impact him and his team including day-to-day responsibilities and nature of work, whether he and/or his team will continue, what they will get and what they are likely to lose. Any beating around the bush on these aspects will only heighten anxiety. Of course, the way an employee receives this information will also be influenced by his age and family situation, health, financial and education challenges, his perceptions about the marketability of his skills and credibility of his front-line supervisor.

One of the best ways to ensure the success of change effort is to treat supervisors as the key link pin in communication process and direct major effort towards regular briefings of these supervisors, who in turn communicate the message to front-line employees one-on-one. Larkin and Larkin say: 'All the resources previously spent communicating indiscriminately are aimed at communicating with supervisors, who are given information, influence, and thereby increased power and status. As a result, they are more likely to help implement change.'[36]

David Leonard and Claude Coltea from *Gallup* assert that *70 per cent* of all change initiatives fail because change agents overlook the role front-line managers play in the success of the initiative.[37]

It is, therefore, necessary that the front-line supervisors have a detailed idea about how the change will manifest on the ground and are fully trained to handle anxieties without giving vague answers.

The other major source information, credible or otherwise, is top management. The top management alone should address issues related to why change is necessary and how it aligns with the organization's need to survive and prosper in a changing environment as well as what are the consequences if the organization does not embark on the change process. Naturally, it is assumed that the top management will have the necessary trust and credibility to be taken as face value. This will be coloured by employees' perceptions of past announcements and how they panned out. If the management has not been mindful of the impact of their decisions and actions in the past, any communication howsoever genuine will be taken with a pinch of salt, to say the least.

Since the way an employee seeks to validate whatever information he gets from the supervisor and the top management from his reference groups, the role of influencers and opinion builders also becomes important. They also need to be taken on board.

The management not only needs to be clear how the information is disseminated through them, front-line supervisors and influencers, but also be mindful of how the information is being perceived on real-time basis. In case of any 'noise', blockade or filtering, remedial actions need to be taken in time.

During the normal course of work in Mega Corporation, there would not be much of interaction between supervisors and workers and all work-related problems were handled through the union leaders. Similarly, the union leaders who were briefed about the changing scenario during the presentations, training programs and negotiations, were themselves opposed to change due to their own vested interests. Circulars had only a limited impact due to low credibility and lack of trust in management. The error committed in this case was of not involving the front-line supervisors in the communication process, thinking that a majority of them had no supervisory potential, having been promoted from workers category, based on seniority. In fact, the first word employees hear about change should come from the person to whom they are close with on a day-to-day basis: their supervisor.

So it was decided to communicate to workers through managers, through union and through circulars. Managers were trained to communicate with the workers, thinking that they come in direct contact with them on day-to-day basis and based on their working relationship, would be able to develop awareness about the changing scenario and support for change, and forgetting that there was a wide gap between the workers and the managers.

Peter Senge has a word of caution:

When communicating with people about new ideas and new business practices, it is not necessary to absolutely convince them. It is important to help them see that the story you are telling is 'on their side', and therefore worth listening to. It need not align perfectly with their point of view. But it needs to show that their point of view is treated fairly, and that they are not cast as outsiders.[31]

As mentioned in chapter 11 (Designing Change Strategy), employees need to be engaged in the process from the initial stages. It is not necessary to be ready with change plan and strategies before starting communication. We can start communicating about the need for change and the risk of not changing. This would keep the employees involved from the earliest stage and a party to the evolution of thought. Since change is personal, it is important to connect with people on a personal level, which will help them address concerns they might have about the impact of change.

CHAPTER 15

Culture of Learning and Innovation Helps

An organization's ability to learn, and translate that learning into action rapidly, is the ultimate competitive advantage.

—Jack Welch

When Microsoft Enterprise Services wanted to enhance its credibility in its Change Management services as a competitive advantage, it partnered with Prosci to create a community of change practitioners and subject-matter experts through extensive training. This training ultimately covered 25,000 employees across the entire Microsoft organization, creating 2,250+ certified change management practitioners.

Oshkosh Corporation, a Fortune 500 company manufacturing toughest specialty trucks, deployed Prosci's change management technology and got its managers trained through a series of role-based trainings for successful management of change.

Likewise, every successful story of change management worldwide is also a story of how seriously change management training was taken as a vital component. For example, GSK got 1,250+ managers certified as essentially change management practitioners.

Training initiative at Mega Corporation was planned keeping in mind the objectives of creating awareness about the business environment, sharing the vision of change, aligning various sources of energy, overcoming the sources of resistance, developing effective teams, evolving right attitudes and values and enhancing the level of motivation and competencies. It was felt that management of change involves multilevel exercises that required involving employees across all the hierarchies, that is, managerial and non-managerial staff. This involvement produces both vertical and horizontal interactions, which need functional as well as behavioural skills of leadership and communication.

Various programs were accordingly organized for operations heads, functional heads, divisional heads, line managers, personnel managers, union executive and the negotiation team. These programmes were not off-the-shelf training programmes but were designed to meet the unique cultural and behavioural requirements of large-scale change at Mega Corporation in particular. Education that supports organizational change differs substantially from education that supports individual development, and thus, the focus of all these efforts was on the development of competencies and widespread skills needed for coping effectively with change. The programs also aimed at giving an understanding of the need for change and how it was going to affect structure, systems, processes and people. Employees were given opportunity to practice the new behaviours in simulated situations that would occur during the change process.

Initially, two trainers were engaged to conduct these programs. One was an expert of contemporary trends in production, implementation and innovation happening around the world. The other was oriented towards Indian ethos and value-based management. The selection of the trainers was based on two central considerations, namely the new ambient and emerging culture and the human response, which considers the characteristics of Indian psyche that govern behavioural patterns. After a few sessions with these trainers, it was felt that their orientation was rather mechanistic, with quick fixes that lacked the sincerity for a deep-rooted and long-term success of the initiative. It was imperative to have trainers with long-term vision and sensitivity to the cultural grounding of the trainees. From there on, well-trained internal faculty conducted all the programmes.

In the case of AG Corporation also, various training programs were organized for different levels of employees to inculcate desired behavior and honing personal skills necessary to implement the change process. These initiatives helped in creating a learning environment in the organization and a supportive climate for change. All other capabilities come alive when the learning capability is nurtured. And it was all happening right here at AGC.

Organizational change cannot take place without learning. How can an organization improve without first learning something new? Change requires doing things differently, which needs new attitudes, ideas, values and skills. New competencies such as knowledge of business as a whole, analytical skills and interpersonal skills are necessary to identify and find a solution to problems. It also requires the ability to see things in alternate ways and displacement of concepts in order to gain new insights. Solving a problem, introducing a product, and re-engineering a process all require seeing the world in a new light and acting accordingly. In the absence of learning, individuals simply repeat old practices. For change to take place, people must start doing things and behaving differently. Change and learning, thus, being intimately related, our aim should be to develop an organizational climate which has the capacity to learn. Well-known management consultant

M. B. Athreya declares, 'Not only will the global market reward learning handsomely; it will severely punish the lack of learning.'

Only the most productive companies are going to win. If we cannot sell a top-quality product at a competitive price, we are going to be out of the game. The companies that survive in times to come will be those that are able to respond quickly and effectively to changing environmental needs. Be it manufacturing or service industry, developing and delivering products or services requires higher skill levels. An organization's competitiveness will get exhibited not only in its ability to source raw materials, cheap capital or skilled hands, but also in its ability to acquire, enhance, share and leverage relevant and new knowledge. We will have to develop capabilities like being adaptive, flexible and responsive, and will have to learn and act at a faster rate than our competitors.

The continually changing world of business requires strategies for sustaining organizational competence, which could lead to newer insights and more integration within the organization. An important question is not about 'doing things right', but about 'doing the right things'. Whether it is development of people in organizations, the improvement of customer service or improving the bottom line, each one involves new ways of doing things, and success depends upon our ability to create new capacities for such action. Only a continuous process of learning can bring this to fruition. Alvin Toffler says that, 'Illiterates of the 21st century will not be those who cannot read and write, but those who cannot learn, unlearn and relearn.'[38]

Only 60 of the top 500 Fortune companies in the United States have maintained themselves on the list from 1955 to 2017. What causes an organization to fail can best be explained by their inability to change when required to maintain their position of strength. They lacked the decisiveness to make the tough decisions that were needed in the changing business environment.

Highlighting the importance of learning, Bhishma, in his advice to Yudhishthir and Pandavas on his deathbed, said that leadership needs an education for itself. There ought to be a good deal of self-analysis and direction towards what is the duty of the model king (leader). The only duty the king (leader) has to do is to continuously renew himself towards his duty.

Nilakant and Ramnarayan view training as an important tool for managing the change process:

Training has become an important tool of OD for communicating and involving employees in the change process. Training programs are also used to generate ideas and develop collaboration among employees from different departments. Training focuses not merely on skills, but also on the development of new roles, new systems, new procedures and new work methods. Training workshops and conferences represent the initial steps in organizational change process. They raise the consciousness of participants, make people aware of the gaps between reality and ideals, provide a common platform to articulate shared problems and difficulties, generate ideas for change, and create greater awareness for change.[8]

Training focuses on honing personal skills in managing change, that is, the skills necessary to implement the change process such as leadership skills, conflict management skills, skills of a change agent, effective communication and so on. Employee training can set the supportive climate for change management when it is competency driven, the competencies the company needs.

Not Through Training Alone

Learning is not through training alone. In fact, classical understanding is that 70 per cent learning is on the job, 20 per cent is through mentoring and only 10 per cent is through formal training. T. V. Rao states:

Much of the learning in organizations is informal, incidental, anecdotal or event-based, cognitive, reactive and could be negative. It is informal because there are few planned learning spaces created for it by organizations. It is based on incidents and anecdotes because of this informal nature. When an incident occurs, the learning takes place. Organizational life is full of events and problems.... Some learning takes place in the process of problem solving. ....It should be planned by creating learning spaces. At present the only learning space that is formally available is the training programs. Every meetings, discussion and interaction between two or more people can be made as a learning space, provided such attitude is inculcated and a learning culture developed.[39]

In AG Corporation, the process of learning was created through sharing of experiences in the weekly review meetings, conducted by the executive director. Everyone would share his experience, be it a success story or failure or any important development related to product, customer, process and so on. Work life is full of events and problems, and every incident could be a source of learning. Gradually, these weekly review meetings became important forums. Problems and issues highlighted during the experience sharing were openly discussed and issues were confronted rather than put under the carpet. This not only encouraged the team members to express ideas, opinions and views but the process was institutionalized as a great learning opportunity. It was also obligatory for members to share their success and failure stories during reviews, irrespective of whether they were small or big wins. This proved to be the most effective platform of learning.

Learning from Failures

Each one learns from the experiences and best practices of others, remaining fully informed of developments throughout. Great learning takes place while sharing the cases of failure, which lead us to insight and better understanding. *Failure is the best teacher, provided we are willing to learn from it.* Such learning, when spread throughout the establishment, becomes organizational learning.

With a sustained attitude, this learning turns into the established way of doing things, almost like a culture woven into the fabric of the organization.

Hubler[40] talked about four constructs as integrally linked to organizational learning: Knowledge acquisition, information distribution, information interpretation and organizational memory. Learning need not be conscious or intentional. An entity learns if, through its processing of information, the range of its potential behaviours is changed.

For developing a learning culture, it is necessary that the corporate environment is supportive and conducive to learning. Learning will only occur in a receptive environment. An environment where innovative ideas and instinctive values are honoured, originality is respected and people are not questioned for their bona fide decisions, where people are encouraged to give their ideas and opinions, where there is collaboration and teamwork, where innovative ideas do not die in the originator's mind and where intuitive values are honoured are the key prerequisites towards creating an organizational climate of learning.

Taking this construct further, Peter Senge[41] popularized the concept of learning organization as 'an organization that is continually expanding its capacity to create its future'.

Underlining this as a key to success in the present context, Bill Gates[42] says:

> Knowledge is becoming the critical success factor in most businesses. Learning organizations that allow employees to pick up new knowledge and innovate constantly are obviously the ones that will generate a sustainable competitive advantage. The successful companies are typically the ones that learn to think differently from the herd, process information more intelligently, come to different conclusions and make different decisions to move ahead of competitors.

The spirit of the learning organization comes from the continuous learning of people, and success comes to those who master the art of this continual and rapid learning. It is also important that organizations embed this knowledge into their systems and processes. This ensures that change is eventually managed in an environment that is now aware, knowledgeable and capable.

However, converting an organization into a learning organization is not a short-term project. Nilakant and Ramnarayan emphasize:

> Attitudes, values and behavior have to be cultivated slowly and steadily over a period of time. An appropriate climate for learning needs to be created. This includes training people in appropriate skills related to problem solving, brainstorming, statistical analysis, conducting experiments and so on. Creation of cross-functional teams, rotation of people across departments and rewarding collaborative behavior, are some of the ways to promote learning across departments.[8]

The first step taken by Mega Corporation was to set sight on a standard of attainment, based on the best practices and norms in the industry. Information and data were collected on best practices and various other parameters, especially from organizations with whom the company competed for business. The core group then went through the process of analysing the data, measured gaps and completed the benchmarking. Benchmarking enables us to seek out the best standard set in everything that the company does. It offers a goal that is attainable. Benchmarking is not primarily a data gathering exercise. More important than the comparative data are the underlying processes that produce that great data. Good benchmarking analysis produces two types of information: quantitative data to measure performance and to set future targets; and qualitative information on the key success factors that explain how the benchmarked company became the best.

Change management involves several sets of players—people who visualize and inspire the change, people who facilitate change and people who execute the change, as well as people who monitor, measure and keep the change rolling.

At Mega Corporation, it was also considered necessary that all those involved in change should be communicated the findings from the benchmarking exercise so that they could re-examine the overall strategy in light of what is 'best peer standard', and incorporate these new learnings into the strategy. A one-day workshop was organized for all the business divisions before initiating negotiations with the union. This was attended by key line managers, finance, HR and marketing personnel, besides the members of the core group. Operation heads first made a presentation about the business-specific strategy for change, which was later juxtaposed with the information about best practices and benchmarks. The very idea of the workshop was to share the information, build enthusiasm and support in the cross-functional team involved in change process. Various cross-functional teams were also constituted for redesigning business process, tackling critical issues of existing incentive schemes and division-specific business issues. There was a need to bridge the gap between the existing abilities that the members of the cross-functional teams possessed and the abilities they needed to perform these tasks—such as self-directed leadership, self-motivated teamwork and self-generated creativity. Various training programmes were, therefore, designed and organized to bridge this gap.

Innovation

Today, the battle is for speed and innovation, as top quality and competitive pricing are not enough, and we need new ideas and new processes that should enable us to win customers. Speed of response to the customer is, thus, becoming a critical factor in the competitive marketplace. Innovation is a critical factor when it comes to being competitive. We need new skills and expertise or have to apply the existing skills in a more efficient manner.

Innovation is not just about developing new products and services; it requires people to do something different and in different ways, in order to create added value. It is about discovering new ways to create and capture value through non-traditional approaches and converting problems into opportunities. Innovation does not always involve new products, services or business model. Sometimes it can be as simple as a new slogan or a new marketing message.

Innovation means uncommon sense, which in turn, is a mindset that seeks to create and unlock new value by challenging prevailing rules of the market. It is a constant process of analysing the market, identifying gaps, understanding the organization's capabilities to deliver on those and maintaining a really close relationship between marketplace and the organization. A truly innovative company never stops encouraging its stakeholders, particularly employees, asking them fundamental questions about its successful products, exploring possibilities or even imagine a completely new product/service. Such companies discover and utilize their special capabilities, which help them deliver products and services better than the competitor does.

Innovation does not mean new products and technologies alone. It could quite possibly be change in organizational culture or change in the way we work and so on. *It is always more than a creative thought or creativity.*

Operational improvements should not be confused with innovation. Efforts for operational excellence or improvements refer to achieving higher performance by reducing errors, lowering costs and avoiding delays but without fundamentally changing how the work gets accomplished. Innovation requires ability to look at problems from different perspective and come out with a larger number of solutions and entirely new ways of working. It is the ability to restructure the problem differently and to discover unconventional ways to unlock the new value.

Innovation is not something we can switch on and off. We need a culture for innovation so that it sustains and remains useful. The commitment of the CEO is essential for creating a culture of innovation. The CEO must meet rank and file, get ideas, involve people and create a culture of openness to ideas. He must be dedicated to innovation and its power and emphasize its importance in all his communications. Though the commitment of the CEO is essential for creating a culture of innovation, it would be wrong to say that only CEO should create innovation. Innovation has to be one of the key responsibilities of every employee, and the company must embed it as an organizational capacity.

Talking about the importance of innovation, N. R. Narayana Murthy[43] says, 'I have always believed that today it is not that the big that eat the small. It is the agile one that eats the latter. It is the innovative one that eats the slow learners.'

Many a time, companies avoid innovation in order to push profitability. In such cases, the obvious result is failure, as happened with Kodak, which failed to embrace change in the market. People within Kodak tried to draw company leader's attention to the world of digital cameras evolving outside the company. Company leaders thought that the world of digital cameras was not as attractive as the world of film sales and that nothing would change. They failed to 'bring the outside in', and we all know how the story ended. Companies must see the threats on the horizon and focus on innovation to avoid inevitable disaster.

For promoting a culture of innovation, it is necessary that organizations measure and reward employees for innovation-related activities. Employees who implement a new idea should be rewarded higher than an employee who does a good job with conventional mindset.

While leadership is characterized as the catalyst for change, innovation is the process that brings in new methods and ideas resulting in required changes. Most managers focus on making existing processes—the status quo—work a little better. Change leaders are much more likely to challenge assumptions, lead the innovation agenda, build space for individuals to innovate and create a culture that inspires people to take risk.

Creative thinking leads to innovation. In fact, it is the pre-requisite for change. We look for new strategies, creative and realistic solutions during the process of change. Innovation and creative thinking is, thus, the key to any successful change effort. One of the key ingredients for a culture of innovation is freedom to make genuine mistakes and failures.

Based on Rajan's experience of working in Japanese multi-national companies, implementing a programme of Japanese International Cooperation Agency and LEAD Innovation Management GmbH Paper by Franz Emprechtinger,[44] the following steps can be adopted to establish a culture of innovation:

1. Management has to set measures and accents so that there is organization-wide awareness. People must be aware of culture of kaizen particularly in Japanese and other organizations inspired by them. Participation is voluntary, and all employees are eligible. They are also provided necessary skills, resources and structures, including reporting procedure, reward system and so on.
2. Communication and promotion have to be year-round. So should be its progress reporting a part of every major meeting year-round. In between, special campaigns can also be launched, including innovation day, innovation festival and so on.
3. In the very beginning, targets can be quantitative but evaluation has to be qualitative.
4. Training on innovation processes and tools is frequently organized with voluntary participation subject to prior notice.
5. There are specific designated colourful innovation spaces with free access on roster basis.
6. Create innovation competition.
7. Reserve innovation budget, including special training as one of the incentives.

CHAPTER 16

90 Per Cent of Change Management Is People Management

Those who have changed the universe have never done it by changing officials, but always by inspiring the people.

—Napoleon Bonaparte

We must remember the most critical principle of change management: organizations do not change, people do. For change to succeed in any organization, each individual is important; she must make her own transition and must think, feel, contribute or do something different. As Kanter puts it, 'Change is always a threat when done to people, but an opportunity when it is done by people'. Change in attitudes leads to change in individual behaviour and changes in individual behaviour, replicated by many people, will result in organizational change. This, in turn, positively impacts performance and quality, which are actually the root intents of any change intervention.

Pfeffer says that people are the principal source of competitive advantage for organizations in the current environment. 'In the past, firms achieved superiority over their rivals through product and process technology, protected or regulated markets, access to financial resources and economies of scale. These are less important now compared to how an organization manages its people.'[45]

While considering organization change, it will be worthwhile to understand current trends among employees and their preferences, from the point of view of strategies to be adopted:

1. A BCG 2018 study on employees in 197 countries found that though willingness to relocate has come down globally vis-à-vis 2014 to 57 per cent, it is still 90 per cent for Indians. The same study also found that top preferences in India are career development, learning and training opportunities, work–life balance and good relationship with superiors.
2. As of 2017, the estimated share of millennial employees was 46 per cent in India.
3. In common with other South Asian millennials, these millennials are high on technology as well as tradition. However, this generation is highly individualistic, except where it comes forward for social causes when it feels that it can make a difference.
4. Use of contract labour has grown phenomenally in industries, crossing 50 per cent in a majority of industries. Even in white-collar jobs, temping is fast becoming the norm everywhere. They may understandably not align with long-term organizational goals.

We must recognize that change happens only through people. The emotional effects of change need to be understood and considered by all involved in the change process. It aims to touch the last person on the job. Jack Welch[46] says that a company today has to find a way to engage the mind of every single employee. Failure to do so will result in wasted minds and disengagement.

Why are 'people' so important for change? Human being has an infinite capacity to think, to feel, to love, to disapprove and to create. He is all the time guided by his emotions, aspirations, desires, fears and prejudices. This non-business character of the human element greatly influences his behaviour in the business environment where various human factors are at play. Organizational change is about switching off the old mindsets and switching on the new mental models and processes. Organizations must remember that this switching has to take place in the minds of the people. Human being feels secure with his set methods of thinking and operating and fears new codes of behaviour in lesser or greater degrees. Hence, organizations that want its people to contribute with their heads and hearts must understand that the non-business character of human being is of utmost importance to bring in new management style and procedures. Management of change is, therefore, not only rational and empirical management but also emotional management of people.

Elaborating this aspect, Duck asserts:

> The issue isn't whether or not people have negative emotions; it's how they deal with them. In fact, the most successful change programs reveal that large organizations connect with their people most directly through values and that, values, ultimately, are about beliefs and feelings.[47]

Imagine our challenges to align our workforce and contrast this with what Sun Tzu says in his book *The Art of War*, written about 2,500 years ago,

> In order to kill enemy, our men must be roused to anger. For them to perceive the advantage of defeating the enemy, they must also have their rewards, so that all your men may have a keen desire to fight, each on his own account.[48]

The emotions that undermine change include insecurity, anger, arrogance, anxiety, pessimism, cynicism and so on. People change their behaviour and gradually develop facilitating emotions such as optimism, faith, trust, passion, hope and enthusiasm, only when their emotional concerns are addressed and resolved. Instead of giving logical reasons for change, we must present people an emotionally compelling case. In successful change efforts, people find ways to help others see the problems or solutions in ways that influence emotions, not just thoughts. Ultimately, organizational change depends on the way human beings behave and, therefore, change management should be holistic and people focused.

Most people want to identify with the success of their organization and to contribute to society. People get involved and take responsibility only if we tell them how to look at it in new ways and how it is going to improve their world. Any change initiative, no matter how good it may be, shall remain a theoretical ideal unless people commit themselves to the change process. We will have to create a broad base of support for change by integrating and weaving together the vision of many people, scores of viewpoints, sensitivities and insights. We also need to establish a process where we acknowledge and reward people who excel and contribute to making something meaningful.

People Must Commit to Change Vision

Reflecting on 20 years of Leading Change towards more value-based work environments, retired Hanover Insurance CEO Bill O'Brien says, 'what people pressurizing for management to drive cultural change don't understand is: A value is a value only when it is voluntarily chosen'. 'Change can also mean top-down programs like reorganizing, reengineering, and many other RE's.' Because these change programmes are typically imposed from the top, many in the organization feel threatened or manipulated by them—even if they support in principle the intent or rationale behind the management change agenda.

There may be a situation where employees are required to give up some of their interests and where mobilizing support might become difficult but they will have to be assured that the change agenda matches the overall interest of all stakeholders, including their own.

As mentioned earlier, in Mega Corporation, the first step towards a shared vision was by way of involving the operation heads of various business units, the key people, next in command to business heads. The approach of the workshop for operation heads was participative, making them partners in planning and strategy making for change.

Developing a shared vision becomes easier if people participate in planning and implementing the change on the principle that people support what they help to create. Participation also leads to better ideas for change.

> Managing change requires developing change-consciousness among people, especially the main targets of change, the workers in case of Mega Corporation. The workers supported the union, which they perceived as the protector, and had low trust in the management. Change cannot succeed unless there is a critical mass of support, and building that support was a key problem, especially amongst workers.

Hultman[49] enunciates eight reasons why people will support change if:

- It will make their life easier by eliminating unnecessary, tedious or unpleasant work.
- It will result in either some personal gain or a new challenge or opportunity. Risks have to be worth taking.
- If people are convinced that there is a situation of impending bankruptcy, a hostile takeover, or a decline in market share and so on.
- They believe that they are being treated fairly. They trust those responsible for the change.
- They believe the change will work, the time is right for the change and adequate resources have been allocated to the change effort.
- The change is consistent with their values or standards and is important.
- They believe those responsible for the change can be trusted. Even if people do not completely agree with a change, they are more likely to go along with it if they trust those responsible for it. People tend to have confidence in those they trust, and they tend to be suspicious of those they do not.

Successful change also involves the maturity to understand that it is a culmination of successful execution of a series of steps many of whom are in parallel, and not sequential. Unfinished execution of one set of steps can jeopardize the entire change effort. Secondly, some steps, especially as they relate to winning the trust and confidence of the people may take some time depending on the complexity of the situation and the nature of strength of forces arrayed against. Trying to speed up maybe counterproductive, because if the people are left behind, the whole edifice of change may collapse. History of change management is replete with such examples worldwide, particularly in acquisitions and mergers.

CHAPTER 17

Who Is Holding the Reins?

The most critical variable in the change process is the top person's integrity: The change team must have good reasons to trust him, his actions and words must match, he should be sensitive to the needs of change team and should communicate with the change team in an open and honest manner. There has to be total transparency between the CEO and all the members of the change team, without manipulation and duplicity.

A major strength during the whole process of change in Mega Corporation had been the support from the chairperson. However, the general perception was that of a weak management that could not take firm stances or could backtrack without a flutter. This was also one of the major reasons why the managers were frustrated and lost hope to manage the company. It was an uphill task for the core group to keep the boss in line and ensure that he did not lose steam.

Later, when someone shared the people's perspective with the chairperson about his leadership—that he did not tolerate any disturbance in production—and asked as to what made him take a bold and different stand, he responded:

I wanted long term improvement in performance and efficiencies and thus sacrificed short-term gains. I wanted to demonstrate as to how strongly we feel about change and get out of the rut. I would have not succeeded and be in the present day happy situation, if I had not taken the stand. Changing human beings is a difficult process and nothing was possible to achieve without demonstrating that we mean business. You start standing alone then others start standing with you.

Yes, no change was possible in Mega Corporation culture without effective sponsorship from the chairperson. The firm handling of various situations developed tremendous confidence amongst the managers, and the whole cadre became a motivated lot, fully involved in the change process.

Whether the change involves new processes, new job roles, new behaviours, new organization structure or new systems, the top leadership must be present to provide the authority and credibility needed for the change to be successful. Prosci, in its benchmarking studies, has identified three roles for senior leaders in times of change:

- *Participate actively and visibly throughout the project:* Sponsors cannot disappear once they have attended the kick-off meeting. Their sustained presence is necessary to build and maintain momentum for the change.
- *Build a coalition of sponsorship and manage resistance:* The sponsor must mobilize other key business leaders and stakeholders so they can take the change back to their part of the organization.
- *Communicate directly with employees:* Employees want to hear about why a change is important from someone at the top—either at the very top of the organization or at the top of their division. Senior leaders are looked to for messages about why the change is being made and the risks or costs if no change is made.

The role of the sponsor is paramount and a critical contributor to success. Effective sponsorship can mobilize and activate the organization while poor sponsorship can inhibit and delay and even derail the process. An active sponsor lends authority and credibility to the change, establishes commitment and sends a message as to how important the initiative is.

Executive sponsorship ensures that sufficient resources are available, priorities are established between competing initiatives, other senior leaders also sponsor the change in their areas, and employees understand why the change is being made and how the change aligns with the vision of the organization. Lack of effective sponsorship results in increased resistance from employees, slow adoption or rejection of change and loss of credibility.

Story of successful change efforts at AG Corporation is also the story of strong sponsorship of the CEO and his value-based leadership who was personally involved in communicating the change vision through regular meetings with various groups and reviewing the progress at regular intervals. The case of Akash Industries is a typical example of another extreme where the chief executive was all the time advocating change in all his conversations but did nothing to demonstrate his conviction and commitment to change.

The CEO is the organization's chief role model and employees expect him to live up to Mahatma Gandhi's famous edict, 'For things to change, first I must change'. Successful CEOs typically embark on their own personal transformation journey. They invest great effort in visibly and vocally presenting the transformation story. It is a long process, but if we put our face in front of the people, they are encouraged to support and practice the behaviour.

Narayana Murthy's 2002 decision to take on the job title of Chief Mentor at Infosys, for example, meant that he had to reinvent himself because he laid aside his formal managerial (CEO) authority at the same time. He explains, 'You have to sacrifice yourself first for a big cause before you can ask others to do the same.'

The role of the top management is in shaping the vision, purpose and strategy. There will be leaders at all levels in the organization but the top management has to mobilize, direct and coordinate the efforts of leaders at various levels in the organization to achieve enduring change. Employees would also be willing to commit themselves to action if the top management has a clear sense of direction and is able to effectively weave the new organizational reality into the fabric of the company. Because the process of changing the culture of an organization takes time, the top management must make a commitment to the long and demanding work involved.

The top person must create a sense of purpose by way of shaping and embedding in the company a set of shared values, which determine the rationale for which the organization exists. An ambition in terms of goals or targets is not enough. The goals will change as the world around us changes but the core values give an identity to the company and hold the organization together.

In the 2016 edition of Prosci change management study, not only active and visible executive sponsorship was listed as the most important contributor to change management success (three times more than other contributors) but also listed lack of active and visible sponsorship as the most challenging obstacle. Participants also reported that 'a sponsor should come from the correct level within the organization and have sufficient influence to affect the budget and other members of the executive leadership.'[50] If the sponsor does not have control over the systems and people impacted by change, being at a wrong level or from some other part of the organization, sponsorship is ineffective. Change management also suffers if the sponsor leaves or is reassigned to some other project or was invisible or indifferent or did not proceed to build a dominant coalition of stakeholder senior managers. Sometimes, sponsors themselves are not clear about their role and treat this as just another responsibility.

CHAPTER 18

Unleashing the Power of Infantry

There is an anecdote in Ramayana. At one stage in the Rama–Ravana war, Lakshman was hit with a powerful missile and was prognosed to be alive only until the next morning, unless he was administered a herb, Sanjivani, available deep inside the Himalayas. So there was only one night in between, and there being no other possibility, Ram and all the generals and soldiers of his army waited for the inevitable with a heavy heart. Suddenly, Jambwant challenged Hanuman, why was he crying, as he alone was capable of flying thousands of *yojanas* (a unit of distance) in the night and coming back before morning with Sanjivani. Unsure of himself, Hanuman slowly gained confidence at the exhortation of Jambwant, and did the seemingly impossible. This was empowerment.

Empowering Employees

Empowerment is not about giving people new authority, new powers and new responsibilities. It is about letting the people feel that they have the power to effect change, to realize their personal and collective dreams and goals. Empowerment is also the process of removing key hindrances that stop people from acting on the vision, and enables them to think, behave and take decisions and action in an independent and autonomous way.

In short, empowerment is making people feel that YOU/WE CAN DO IT and WE ARE WITH YOU IN THIS. Conger and Kanungo[51] define empowerment as:

> A process of enhancing feelings of self-efficacy among organizational members through the identification of conditions that foster powerlessness, and through their removal by both formal organizational practices and informal techniques, of providing efficacy information. This makes employees much more productive, have higher job satisfaction and feel more committed towards the organizational goal.

'You cannot confer power on human beings. Try liberating them instead', says Oren Harari in *World Executive Digest* of August 1994. He further says that as an effective leader, your job is to create an environment where your people take on the responsibility to work productively in self-managed, self-starting teams that identify and solve complex problems on their own. If you concentrate on doing this, you will find that your people will need you only for periodic guidance and inspiration, which frees you to spend your time confronting the big picture, common-fate sorts of strategic and organizational issues. Concentrate on offering your people the gift of liberation from the shackles of the organizational bureaucracy and from your own 'helpful' instructions. Liberate them from the protectors of the old guard. Do that and those delicious feelings of power will emerge among your people, as will productivity and organizational success.

Autonomy at work cannot be seen in isolation. It should have strong linkages with the management systems and the work culture of the organization. For empowerment to be experienced as 'real', it is essential for the organization to have:

- An appropriate organizational structure allocating responsibilities and accountability at all levels

- Decentralization of power and authority
- Consultative decision-making
- Mutual trust
- Flexibility in operations
- Transparent communications and learning through experimentation

Empowerment is about building accountability and ownership by providing an environment that is free of constraints. Employees will demonstrate wholehearted commitment in achieving organizational goals once their feeling of powerlessness is removed and they are given access to every kind of resource. Empowered and well-informed employees are able to take initiative without the need to appease authority. It is almost like a self-discovery where every individual finds he is capable of holding ownership, without depending on external sanction.

The obstacles and constraints that need to be addressed in order to provide a hurdle-free environment for employees could be system related, like the absence of an evaluation and reward system or absence of economic rewards associated with transformation. There could also be barriers in the mind where employees are aware of the vision but do not act as they lack conviction about the change taking place. Information blockades could also hold back the process, since information is a source of power and lack of it can give a semblance of dis-empowerment. It is important to develop a system of information sharing in the organization. Very often, the leader himself is an obstacle—either an immediate superior or someone higher in authority. Such impediments to the process of change should not be overlooked and cleared in the best possible manner. Besides these, unclear goals and objectives and ambiguity in roles and responsibilities can become a huge barrier too. It is imperative to fine-tune and clearly define every role and every goal at all levels.

Change programmes need to involve not only the leaders as sponsors of change but also the employees who will be affected by the changes to the work environment. The organization has the responsibility to create a work environment that helps foster the ability and desire of employees to act in empowered ways, to an extent that they feel inspired to partner the change process and make it a success.

> A key role of the change facilitator at Mega Corporation was to convince people that not only this change was possible but we can do it despite all odds. This unleashed new energy, especially amongst line managers and front-line HR managers.

Many companies worldwide are turning to what is called 'shadow boards' to solve the twin problem of employee disengagement, especially amongst the younger employees and weak response to changed market conditions. For example, Gucci started a shadow board comprising millennials in 2015. This shadow board has given insights and helped deploy its internet and digital strategies leading to 136 per cent growth in Gucci sales from financial years 2014 to 2018.[52]

A Dolphin, Not a Whale[53]

Torben Rick, propagating the dolphin versus whale concept, says that organizational change should be divided into a series of short steps or phases, something similar to how dolphins breathe. Belonging to the same family, a whale breathes after long intervals (see Figure 18.1).

We need to be cognizant of the fact that real transformation takes time. Most people will not go on the long march unless they see compelling evidence within a few months that the journey is producing expected results.

Creating Small Wins

Achieving a long-term goal or a major breakthrough is relatively arduous. Even small wins or incremental progress can boost work life tremendously, increase people's engagement with their work, and can have a major impact on people's sense of well-being.

Figure 18.1. Change Management Is a Dolphin, Not a Whale

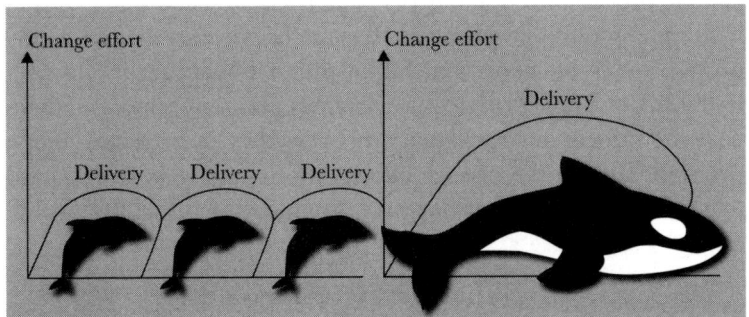

Source: https://www.torbenrick.eu/blog/change-management/change-management-is-a-dolphin-not-a-whale/

Providing clarity and clearing the uncertainty about the management's role with regard to taking tough stands also inculcated tremendous confidence amongst line managers who were earlier highly demoralized. As the line managers witnessed the clear signals and firm stances taken by the management, they gradually became more involved. The small wins help build necessary momentum and provide evidence that sacrifices are worth it.

In Mega Corporation, the tasks and processes were clearly laid out for the core working team. There was a high sense of ownership and commitment along with complete faith in joint efforts. The unified and well-coordinated actions of the core group helped the firm successfully handle two major agitations, demonstrating its commitment to change and thereby sending the right signals. In the past, all business heads were managing their departments independently. There was singular and short-term vision to achieve results without any coordination. This had resulted in serious disparities in policies and practices and the union was taking advantage of this situation. The unified actions of the management during agitations clearly conveyed its commitment to change, thereby improving the level of commitment for change, especially amongst managers.

Creating short-term wins is an important step for a successful change process. Even in our personal lives, we need small wins to maintain emotional well-being. Research indicates that a notable proportion of incidents that had a minor impact on the project had a major impact on people's feelings about it. Similarly, these wins are critical in the change process as they provide credibility, promote faith in the change effort, emotionally reward the hard work, keep the critics at bay and provide impetus to the overall effort.

Celebrating success and small wins became a regular feature at the beginning of all monthly communication and review meetings chaired by CEO in AG Corporation. Top team and managers felt that changes are quite visible in the attitude of people and things were moving in the right direction. They became optimistic about the future of the company and motivated their departments with renewed zeal.

The change team should focus first on tasks where they can quickly achieve unambiguous, visible and meaningful results. This will keep the organization moving forward, reducing anxiety that can get fixated on problems that are too large to handle immediately. Many small wins are necessary to achieve our larger goal of change. These wins reaffirm the faith of change leaders about the validity of their vision and strategies, serve as a great motivating factor to those actively involved in achieving the vision and energize work life tremendously.

During the process of change, those sceptically sitting on the fence start kindling faith in the efforts and begin to help once they witness the success of small efforts. Level of resistance comes down and momentum builds after the first wins, as changes get consolidated one after the other. Even ordinary, incremental progress can increase people's engagement and their happiness during the work.

After first few short-term wins, change efforts get a definite direction as well. We should build on this energy to make the vision a reality by keeping the sense of urgency heightened and rewarding/ recognizing the staff that have made a difference. Remember, these wins should not get to our head and the temptation of declaring victory prematurely has to be controlled.

Short-term wins nourish faith in the change efforts, emotionally reward the hard work, bring impetus and help us appreciate the many milestones that exist on the path to making sustainable change. These wins provide both, positive feedback to change leaders and concrete data about the validity of their vision and strategies. They also help retain the essential support of bosses, justifying the much-needed reinforcement, and keep us fresh and motivated for the next challenging situation ahead leading up to the long-term goal.

It is critical for teams and individuals working on complex change process to achieve small wins regularly. Setbacks are quite common in handling complex problems, and people can get disheartened with setbacks unless they touch and feel some meaningful progress, even if that progress is a small one. This brings about a feeling of accomplishment and a sense of optimism, nudging them towards behavioural changes. Those who have worked hard to create the wins are re-energized as well. Those who have been pessimistically or sceptically sitting on the sidelines begin to help. Quick performance improvements undermine the efforts of cynics, they make less disruptive noise and the vision begins to seem real.

PART V

LEADERSHIP: THE X FACTOR OF SUCCESSFUL CHANGE FACILITATION

CHAPTER 19

Leadership and the Need for a Change Leader

Effective and meaningful change will have to be led by a group of people but not necessarily by the vision of a single leader. Udai Pareek[54] remarks on this present-day leadership trend; 'we are now in a century of great leadership. By contrast, the 20th century was a century of great leaders. We will need effective leaders in large numbers at all levels in all organizations, rather than only a few great leaders.'

We hardly find a real agreement on the definition of leadership. It is basically exercising influence through a pattern of behaviour that arouses involvement and commitment in people around. In most successful cases where the level of involvement is high, people know what they are doing and why. Leadership is, thus, a process of locating and nurturing infinite possibilities in human beings and affecting and remoulding people's behaviour. Leadership is also interlaced with the essential function of inculcating and shaping a refreshed work culture.

John Maxwell says:

Leadership is influence—nothing more, nothing less. The greater the impact you want to make, the greater your influence needs to be. Managers can maintain direction, but they can't change it. To move people in a new direction, you need influence. If you can't influence others, they won't follow you. And if they won't follow, you are not a leader. The leadership is, thus, about influencing people to follow.[55]

According to Lao-Tzu, China's most influential political ruler in the 5th century BC, the best form of leadership is to be conscious of the leadership potential within the followers and to let them unleash this potential in a spontaneous way. He says that the highest level of ruler is the one who leads without words, allowing the people to follow their own natures and live their own lives.

Azim Premji, one of the most successful business leaders, has given 10 steps to leadership. These are as follows:

• First, leaders must develop powerful personal credibility. This means they should not only be consistent in what they say and do but must deliver on their commitments. The leader has to generate collective enthusiasm in the team, and the team must have faith in the leader before they commit to his dream. Personal credibility is the most important ingredient of leadership.

• Second, great leaders tell people clearly what they expect from them, whether in terms of performance or values. The more that is expected from people, the more they tend to deliver. Low expectations can lead to low ambition and hence low performance. Winning leaders are demanding leaders. They demand discipline, accountability and continuous increase in performance and productivity.

• Third, great leaders are great teachers and coaches. Expectations alone are not enough. Neither are rewards and punishments. People need guidance on the path they need to follow. This does not mean that the leader should spoon-feed his people. It only means that the leader must have the capacity to look ahead and give the right amount of guidance at the right time, and thus be available for his people.

• Fourth, successful leaders need to have energy and be able to energize others. Leadership demands extraordinary physical, mental and spiritual energy to remain on top of the demands made on them. Leaders must work both hard and smart, long and intensely.

- Fifth, leaders do not always have to be in the limelight. One has to realize that leadership is not a privilege but a responsibility. Think of birds flying in a formation. At different times, different birds lead the formation. The leader must know where to lead and where to step back.
- Sixth, winning leaders face reality. They do not dither. Leadership is about making tough 'yes–no' decisions. Winning leaders are willing to decide with imperfect data, if needed, because leadership is about making judgements that others are either unwilling or unable to make.
- Seventh, leaders keep renewing themselves. They constantly learn from their own experiences and those of others. They create knowledge, capturing and sharing processes and methods in the organization.
- Eighth, leaders surround themselves with people who err on the side of optimism. If people are always in the company of cynics, they will soon find themselves becoming like them. A cynic knows all the reasons why something cannot be done. Instead, leaders spend time with people who have a 'can do' approach. They choose their advisers and mentors correctly.
- Ninth, leaders play to win. Playing to win is not the same as cutting corners. When you play to win, you stretch yourself to your maximum and use all your potential. It also helps you to concentrate your energy on what you can influence instead of getting bogged down with the worry of what you cannot change. Leaders do their best and leave the rest.
- Tenth, leaders respect themselves. Without self-confidence, it is impossible to lead. This is needed even more in conditions of uncertainty and change. In Wipro, one of the leadership qualities on which we measure our leaders year after year is self-confidence.

Swami Vivekananda says:

> The best leader is one who leads like the baby. The baby, though apparently depending on everyone, is the king of the household…. It is absolutely necessary to the work that I should have the enthusiastic love of as many as possible,

while I myself remain entirely impersonal. Otherwise jealousy and quarrels would break up everything. A leader must be impartial.'[15]

Another interesting perspective is given by Vallabh Bhai Patel: 'If it becomes necessary for us to sit in seats of authority, let our hands be clean, our tongue mild, our hearts sound and our vision clear.'

Change Leader

Leaders today have to deal with more uncertainty and ambiguity than ever before, and therefore, must create an organization where all levels of hierarchy adopt a common vision and contribute in achieving it. Leaders should make sure that people not only see the vision, they live and breathe it. They need to influence and persuade people to reflect on and change their mental models. Change leaders do not bring change; they facilitate its emergence and mobilize support to the idea of change. They need to have the skills for influencing others.

Morris and Raben, while referring to role of leader in change, feel that:

> There are number of specific things that leaders can do. First, they can serve as models. Through their behavior, they can provide a vision of the future state and a source of identification for different groups within the organization. Second, leaders can serve an important role in articulating the vision of the future state. Third, they can play a crucial role in rewarding key individuals and specific types of behavior. Fourth, they can provide support through political influence and needed resources. Similarly, leaders can remove roadblocks and maintain momentum through their public statements. Finally, leaders can send important signals through the informal organization.[28]

Effective change management requires credible and visible leadership that helps people unlock their potential, change their behaviour and hold everyone accountable. When we talk of behaviour, we are talking about values, attitudes and beliefs, which form an important component of the organization culture. In view of each individual's own family, educational, experiential and psychological background, it is the leader's task to unify, motivate and develop commitment amongst individuals towards the change mission and be a real transformational leader. Organization-wide change requires sustained efforts, and the role of leadership is to ensure continued momentum in the change efforts.

Nadler[56] defines the key challenges of leadership as follows:

1. Strategic anticipation. Correctly anticipating at least strategic direction the world, the environment and the industry will take is sine qua non for visioning the future of the organization.
2. Sense of Urgency. Some urgency is needed to stimulate behaviour.
3. Effective creation and management of pain. Pain, however, can motivate both functional and dysfunctional behaviour. Again, only the leadership has the capacity both to create pain and shape the responses to it.
4. Making people believe that reorientation is truly critical to the core issues of the organization.

True leaders have a compelling vision of a new future and get followers committed to it by shaping their values, interpreting the organizational purpose and by empowering them. They get things done through commitment, by keeping the fire burning within people. When Reliance Patalganga refinery was completely submerged in the flash floods of 1989, DuPont managers declared that it was virtually impossible to get the project back on track in less than four months. But the company's chairperson, Dhirubhai Ambani knew something more—that nothing was impossible if his employees were motivated. As the foreign consultants looked on, every single employee worked round the clock, sweeping the floor, dismantling the machines and cleaning them, restoring the refinery back to shape in less than three weeks. Being associated with the company during the period, Dr Arora was a witness to the commitment of the great leader and how he motivated people to complete the job in record time, to the astonishment of advisers from DuPont. Change leaders create hope, excitement and engagement, inspiring people to make things happen.

These change leaders encourage risk-taking and have a relatively high tolerance for mistakes made by followers. In situations of complex change, it is vital that leaders trust others to bring their own perspectives to the table. Trusting others means allowing them to perform their task without micromanaging them. Leaders encourage and seek out innovative solutions and approach old situations with new perspectives.

Jon R. Katzenbach[57] has given common characteristics of change leaders:

1. *Commitment to a better way:* Real change leaders see their target as exciting, worthwhile, and essential to their personal satisfaction, as well as to the prosperity of the institution.
2. *Courage to challenge existing power bases and norms:* Real change leaders do not welcome failure, neither do they fear it. By demonstrating the ability to rise again, they also build courage in those around them.
3. *Initiative to break through established boundaries:* Real change leaders take it upon themselves to work with others to solve unexpected problems, break bottlenecks, challenge the status quo and think outside the box. Setbacks never discourage them from trying again and again.
4. *Motivation of themselves and others:* Highly motivated themselves, real change leaders create energy, excitement and momentum in the people around them.
5. Provide opportunities for others to follow their example and take personal responsibility for change. More often than not, they use facts about customers and competitors to motivate their people to win in the marketplace.
6. *Caring about how people are treated:* Real change leaders are fair minded and intent on enabling others to succeed. They never deliberately manipulate or exploit people. They are determined to help each person achieve their full performance potential.

7. *A sense of humour:* Far from trivial, a sense of humour often gets real change leaders through when those around them have lost heart. It enables them to help others stay the course in the face of confusion, discouragement and the occasional inevitable failure.

Looking Within: Change Mindset

We have so far discussed leader behaviours which help top leaders be more effective in their role as change leaders. Perhaps, deeper than that is the change and growth mindset. This cannot be developed in a day.

How does one develop this?

First and foremost, there has to be an instinctive habit of getting out of one's comfort zone. Kouzes and Posner talk about 'Challenging the Status Quo' as the first out of five practices that define leadership.[58]

Second, continuous reading habit, particularly life experiences of those who broke mental barriers, such as Steve Jobs, Jack Welch, Anthony Robbins, Stephen Covey and so on, helps. At the same time, one has to protect oneself from naysayers, lest old dictum of garbage in, garbage out plays out.

Third, essentially believe that hard work, grit and discipline bring more achievements than talent and intelligence.

Fourth, be humble to acknowledge their own as well as others' strengths and contributions.

Mark Sanborn says that change management is the single most important skills of the new millennium.[59] He further asks if the leader is 'change-skilled'. A leader needs to answer the three questions himself:

'Today your playing field can shift from day-to-day. Can you?

Today, your job description could change overnight. Can you?

Today, your employer and manager can change any time? Can you?'

A leader's mindset has to change before he becomes eligible for being an effective change leader. Then alone, he will better appreciate the moment of inertia of a human mind and design humanistic change plan that minimizes resistance.

Lichenstein[60] says that a top leader also needs to ponder over these questions before embarking upon a major change:

1. What are the values and motivations of my board and how do I find them?
2. How do I gain acceptance for policies at the right level?
3. What are the values and motivations of my main stakeholder groups (e.g., staff, suppliers, communities, customers and market analysts)?
4. How do I bring on board these other stakeholders even though our values may be different?
5. How do I use this information to develop better policies and strategies so that I am able to increase shareholder value?

If the values of the top team are at variance with the rest of the organization, even if at unconscious level, it will give rise to the following kinds of responses:

1. 'Management has lost the plot.'
2. 'They are killing the soul of the organization. We did not join this organization to see this day!'
3. 'Why are they in so much hurry?'

As a result, there may be passive and active resistance; even sabotage will not be unlikely, derailing the entire change effort. Therefore, it is the top leader's/team's responsibility to first focus on value alignment at least with the key influencers in the affected population, besides with key stakeholders. At this point, it may be pertinent to reiterate that the effort should be to develop a consensus instead of a majority vote.

CHAPTER 20

Value-based Leadership and Successful Change

The emphasis of traditional leaders is on systems, practices, organization and keeping things under control. Their focus is on control to ensure efficiency, productivity, performance and profits. Traditional leaders seldom make good change leaders because of this restricted and limiting mindset. Value-based leadership looks inward for strength, purpose and values. This enables them to lead others reach their full potential, thereby making a difference in qualitative besides quantitative performance. Value-based leadership promotes personal and organizational vision, enabling people to make complex decisions required in today's environment.

There are two stories of Mr G. D. Birla, an Indian entrepreneur of a bygone era. He once declined a proposal to manufacture lac because he was told that the process involved killing of insects. On another occasion, he was approached by Mr M. M. Malviya for donation to his dream project of setting up Banaras Hindu University. While waiting in the anteroom of Mr Birla's chamber at his residence, Mr Malviya heard Mr Birla shouting at his son for spoiling many matchsticks in lighting a candle. Gravely disappointed at Mr Birla's stingy behaviour, Mr Malviya tried to make a quiet exit without asking for donation. Meanwhile, Mr Birla called for Mr Malviya. Mr Malviya came back and after great hesitation, told Mr Birla the purpose of his visit. Mr Birla happily gave him a cheque for a handsome amount and asked him more about plans of the university. By now, Mr Malviya had become comfortable and with Mr Birla's permission, he told him about his getting disappointed by conversation between Mr Birla and his son. Mr Birla had a good laugh and said that just because he had a lot of money, he could not allow waste by his son even in a small thing. The success of the leader depends on backing up his words with actions as this creates trust. The only way for a leader to create trust is by laying out values and then walking the talk. It is authenticity and the character that builds trust and makes value-based leadership possible. Since character is a combination of integrity, selflessness, understanding, conviction, courage, loyalty and respect, the sum total of our values and beliefs, it invariably gets reflected in our behaviour and actions. It is a pattern of behaviour, thoughts and feelings based on universal principles of moral strength, and integrity—plus the courage to live by these principles each day. This high character is what makes people believe in you and look up to you as a leader.

Warren Wilhelm (1996) stresses the importance of values as guiding principle of leadership thus:

> As the pace of change in our world continues to accelerate, strong basic values become increasingly necessary to guide leadership behavior. Such values act as social constructs. They allow leaders to make decisions about the direction in which to lead and how to proceed. Without values, otherwise effective leadership can be grossly destructive socially, as proved by dictators such as Hitler and Saddam Hussein. It is the interactive combination of intelligence and sound social values that allows leaders to nudge forward the positive progress of humankind.[61]

David Hurst (1995) says that 'Organizational change requires not means-end rationality but value-based rationality. In value-based rationality, action is taken not because it is a means to achieve certain technical goals but because the action is seen as intrinsically valuable.'[62]

Noel M. Tichy,[63] a distinguished professor and consultant, while emphasizing the importance of values, has observed that winning leaders deliberately and consciously do five things:

- They clearly articulate a set of values for the entire organization or team.
- They continually reflect on the values to make sure that they are appropriate to achieving the desired goals.
- They embody the values with their own behaviour.
- They encourage others to apply the values in their own decisions and actions.
- They aggressively confront and deal with pockets of ignorance and resistance.

Danah Zohar feels that with value-driven leadership 'business becomes a spiritual vocation in the largest sense of the word, and its leaders serve the wonderful what can be of reality.'[64]

Chanakya has also mentioned, in his *Arthshastra*, that the root of holding a kingdom (organization) lies in the self-controlled life of the ruler (leader). If the ruler follows the dictates of his duty (dharma), the ruled also do the same. If the ruler be un-pious, the ruled are also un-pious. The ruled are simple if the ruler be simple. The ruled follow the ruler.

An excellent exposition of human values is found in the long counselling session, which Bhishma had with Yudhishthira, as given in 'Shantiparva', about the conduct of the king (leader):

- The king's behaviour has to be supported by self-restraint, with passions under control.
- The king, remaining cheerful by meditation and by restraining desire and other passions of the heart, succeeds in obtaining great merits.
- The king has his soul under restraint, is possessed of wisdom, and is desirous of prosperity.
- The king should always reflect upon himself: What does he lack? What evil habits he is addicted with? What are the sources of his weakness? What are the sources of his faults?

- The king—who is free from malice, who has his senses under control and who is gifted with intelligence—thrives in affluence like the ocean swelling with the waters discharged into it by a hundred streams.

Our Indian philosophy of work is that we work not simply to satisfy our physical, mental and psychological needs, but it is an activity directed for the realization of the divine within us, the internal moral consciousness, which helps us behave more honestly and spontaneously, for the good of all. It is an offering to the divine in us to unfold itself. Sri Krishna, in verses 45 and 46 of chapter XVIII of The Gita, has said that devoted to his own duty and worshipping Him, from whom is the evolution of all beings, with one's own duty, man attains perfection.

During the final stages of negotiations at Mega Corporation, serious differences arose on certain points in the draft settlement and both the parties held their ground. Finding no way out to resolve the stalemate, the union agreed to refer these points of differences to an arbitrator, whose decision shall be final and binding. The union opted for the change facilitator (heading management's negotiation team) as arbitrator. The arbitrator heard both the parties and gave his award, which was accepted by all. This clearly proves that a value-based leader, even though he represents the interests of opposite party, could enjoy the trust and confidence of people. The union agreed to accept the change facilitator as an arbitrator because he was considered as trustworthy, fair and compassionate in his individual capacity.

In business, if we dare to speak about values, we are considered preachers and not businessmen who take decisions that make sense from a financial point of view. What is most important is to determine: Have we followed our inner conscience? Have we done what was right? Have we given our best effort? Have we used all of our senses and values that we are conscious and aware of? If we are leading a purpose and we are doing it based on some fundamental values, then we have great potential and we can be successful in almost anything.

Zubin Mulla has written many articles on importance of values. In one of his articles in Aon Hewitt's publication, he says that:

> The most compelling evidence of the importance of values comes from a recent study of 45 Chinese Chief Executive Officers (CEOs) and their direct and indirect subordinates (Fu, Tsui, Jun, & Lan, 2011). The study showed that the CEO's values substantially enhanced the impact of the CEO's behaviours on middle manager's attitudes and behaviour intentions. More specifically, only when CEOs gave more importance to others' happiness as compared to their own happiness, did the CEO's leadership-oriented behaviours have substantial positive effects on middle managers' affective commitment towards the organization and the middle managers' intention to leave the organization.[65]

There are differences in opinion, however. Burns suggests when history evaluates the legacy of a leader, what matters most is not whether they were personally virtuous or ethical in their interactions with others, but whether they had the right intentions and whether they led their followers to a better state or not.[66]

It is not just the values of the CEO that can have a major influence. In one of the organizations perpetually afflicted with industrial relations (IRs) conflict, a new HR head joined. Before him, general IR approach was largely political and people believed that successful IR management means managing power equations between various employee groups, playing one against the other through selective allocation of benefits, hiding data about the health of the organization lest employees/unions may jack up their price for industrial peace, being hand in glove with labour authorities and so on. Incidentally, these beliefs are widespread, especially in manufacturing and other organizations with a large workforce. New HR head was intrinsically opposed to this approach. So, while he played along the then rules of the game, slowly he started being upfront about what was practical and what was not. Naturally, this not only led to consternation amongst other personnel tasked with handling IR and top management, but unions were also flummoxed and smelt a conspiracy to break the power of unions because reverberations of plain speaking also started reaching rank-and-file workers. This was especially so because many of the just expectations of workers were met even before the unions raised a demand. Over the years, conflict and animosity was replaced by harmony and trust and even annual collective bargaining rituals became a tame affair lasting a few hours instead of days earlier. In time, finding himself with no significant work to do on IR front, HR head started devoting himself to employee training, marking a shift in his own career.

PART VI

CULTURE AND VALUES AS VEHICLES OF CHANGE

CHAPTER 21

Influence of Culture and Indian Culture

Culture is the totality of dominant beliefs, guiding norms, understandings, values and ways of thinking that is shared by members of an organization. This is also exhibited via patterned regularity in people's behaviour, manifested in customs and traditions. It represents an environment jointly created by people, leading them to action and coordinated effort, and truly engaging people, without any precise sanction. An essence of the distilled wisdom of generations belonging to a society or organization, culture sets the standards and boundaries of behaviour within and beyond.

Rajagopalachari describes culture as a subtle instrument of civilization, which acts through family training, tradition, religious belief, literature and education. It acts silently. It makes people feel they are not forced to obey but do it of their own free will and gives them a sense of pride in good behaviour.[67]

In any company, people develop particular ways of handling work; gradually this becomes the accepted way of doing things. These ways of doing things become habits, and that is what corporate culture is: the habits that have become part of the organization's personality, or 'how things are done around here', what will be rewarded, what punished and what ignored.

Geert Hofstede has been one of the foremost researchers in this field. He views organizational culture as a collective mental programming and considers that values are its fundamental core. Values are broader, trans-institutional principles that apply to a range of situations. They include the general ideals and standards of the organization.[68]

Unless any major change effort aims at successfully aligning or modifying organization culture to new imperatives, it stands the risk of failure.

A 2013–2014 Change and Communication ROI Study of Towers Watson and Willis across the world found that fundamentals of change levers (leadership, communication, involvement, training/learning and measurement—that are known to drive success) are more effective when grounded in a deep understanding of an organization's culture and workforce. The same study also found that doing the following improves change effectiveness:

- Paying careful attention to employees—evaluating the culture, employee readiness for change and, in particular, the impact of changes on people.
- Training managers to be catalysts for change and holding them accountable.

Global 2015 study of Prosci on Best Practices in Change Management found that:

9 out of 10 respondents rated cultural awareness as either important or very important to change management success. They felt that change management has to be customized for the culture in which it has to be implemented. An understanding of cultural norms allows change managers to integrate change activities more fully thereby increasing credibility. Culture-specific norms and taboos can act as landmines to change itself. Lastly, critical communication improves through culturally-aware translators.

For example, the study found that open forum engagement was not effective in Asian context, because of the inherent employees' hesitation in openly voicing dissent.

Any organization operates in a certain sociocultural milieu and cannot be indifferent to the values of the society in which it operates. The greater the degree of divergence between an organization's culture and the culture of the society in which it operates, the greater the amount of energy that is dissipated in unproductive ways. Even if these differences are not so apparent in day-to-day running of the organizations, these fault lines reappear in the event of any major change, seriously undermining efforts for smooth transition.

In today's world, there are quite a large number of multinational organizations from across the world. These organizations, rooted in their local cultures of the USA, Germany, Korea, Japan, China and so on, often get dismayed by some of the values and practices of Indian managers and employees. Likewise, Indian MNCs operating in other countries often find local cultures to be at variance with their mental models and behaviour patterns, leading to unproductive misunderstandings.

Western research is rooted in what it can be loosely called as Western world view. For example, Research Psychologist Lewis Andrews, after 10 years of investigating the connection between spirituality and mental health, says that study shows that people who believe in one God and have very strong spiritual values are happier, healthier and in most cases more intellectually involved than people who do not.[69] One does not know what are its implications in the Indian context.

Indian Mindset and Culture

Most of the management models are rooted in Western theories and cultural constructs, which may not be consonant with Indian mental models. One of the most visible effects of this incongruence is found in appraisal and reward systems. A 2014 article titled Kill Your Performance Ratings based on a survey by PricewaterhouseCoopers found that 95 per cent of managers were dissatisfied with their performance management systems. Incongruence between policy and practice exacerbated by typical

Indian cultural norm is not bringing up any negative or unpleasant issues in face-to-face interactions with those who work with you, unless you are angry. The same ambivalence has got translated into routine communication about any disciplinary action anywhere in India: 'though your misconduct deserves strict disciplinary action, management is taking a lenient view and you are being let off with (a lighter punishment).' The unwritten value is personal/human relations must extenuate enforcement of discipline. Even the societal value is, 'who are we to punish? God will take care'. This ultimately leads to Indian state being perceived as a soft state.

Alan Roland compares the American and Indian societies thus[70]:

Feature	American Society	Indian Society
Important structures	Peer groups, extra familial relationships	Extended family
Relationships	Cousin, brother in law— generic names	Specific words for each relationship
Occupational and major life decisions	Individual decides	Family has a role
Orientation	Change	Stability

Therefore, we must understand Indian culture and psyche to devise more effective Indian models of leadership and change management.

Spiritualism Is Not Religion

People often confound spirituality with religion. Away from the religious practice, spiritualism is a belief that one's existence is inextricably linked with other beings and even 'non-beings' like nature.

One of the main constructs of Indic philosophy is *Om Ishaavaasyamidam yatkincha jagatyaam jagat* (*Ishopnishad*) meaning, '*God pervades everything—living and non-living.*'

These non-living include vegetation, rivers, mountains, stones and so on, even universe. Associated with this basic perspective, the work ethos in India is based on a holistic vision of life. The end of all work is to bring out the divine in ourselves by serving the divine in others. A person has to work to realize the divine within him; therefore, work is considered as duty (*sadhana*) in Indian philosophy. It is the performance of action for the unfoldment of the spirit towards greater perfection and working for the good of others, good of all being. Somewhere this also connects and builds towards the guiding philosophy of 'Vasudhaiva Kutumbakam', of treating the whole world as one family.

Those with spiritual view to life do not measure success or failure. They follow their inner conscience, do what they consider right, and give their best effort, using all their values and good sense that they are in acceptance of. Spirituality is also paying attention to the inner self, to be able to perfect one's behaviour and attitudes, both inwardly and externally with others, basing one's conduct on fundamental values, such as love, truth, peace and equanimity.

At work, if we have a spiritual outlook, we have a wider outlook; we are more patient and we have greater respect for and better understanding of the people we work with. If we have a righteous policy based on care for people, and a compelling business strategy, then financial success will come automatically.

Influence of the Construct of the Joint Family

Indian culture is predominantly spiritual, with a cosmic vision, leading towards high spiritual truth inside every human being. It does not mean that all the people of India are spiritual. The streets are teaming with shallow and unspiritual lots. But society extends its respects to the spiritually alive people.

Suresh Krishna (1988), Chairperson and Managing Director, Sundaram Fasteners Ltd, says:

In the West, people respect people who achieve, who acquire things, who become richer, who are more successful. In India, people respect those who renounce, who give up things, who are like Swami Vivekananda. These are the people who are respected, not the people who acquire things in life.[71]

Sundaram Fasteners Ltd is one of the most successful companies of the country, with a record of not a single industrial dispute or loss of a single working hour during 30-odd years of its history. Suresh Krishna says that this could be made possible by practising what is very fundamental to Indian ethos: the joint family system.

The institution of joint family has survived centuries and is still a social force influencing the way of life and attitudes of a large majority of Indian people. The binding principles of the joint family have been so strong that numerous foreign influences over the centuries have been unable to dilute its basic structure. The eldest is the head of the joint family and has a stature to reckon with. He/she is the 'kartā'. The welfare of the family is his/her sole concern. He/she is demanding yet affectionate, listens to everyone in the family with equanimity, involves others in decision-making, takes care of their interests, and is always approachable. The kartā's nurturance is reciprocated with respect and reposing of confidence in him/her by the members of the family. What we see around in our societal day-to-day behaviour that we stand up when a senior enters the office, refrain from smoking or drinking alcohol in the presence of an elder or senior, speak humbly and politely to all elders, is all because we have grown up in a system where the head of family and all elders are respected.

While describing primary characteristics of and basic learnings from the joint family, P. Singh and Asha Bhandarkar have mentioned that the individual in the joint family is exposed to warm and close personal relationships, where emotional links with others become the core characteristics of Indian personality profile and the kartā by his/her behaviour and style evokes feelings of security and trust. They have, thus, argued for evolving culturally consistent and relevant management system based on kartā model.[72]

A joint family consists of large number of members and its organization and structure is based on cooperation. It fosters great virtues such as sacrifice, affection, cooperation, spirit of selflessness, broadmindedness and self-control.

The notion that the kartā or the head of the family is omnipotent and over-dominating and puts at risk the individuality of other members in the family does not seem to be correct. Since all the members of the family are bound by the obligations imposed by the sacred laws and customs, every individual enjoys lot of personal freedom, operating within the set of rules.

Indian environment is characterized by a strong sense of value attached to tradition and traditional practices. Indian workers, who are by and large rural, bring to their organizations the cultural norms and values in their most raw form. Hence, there has been a greater penetration of social habits and cultural values into the work environment of organizations. Coming from an environment of strong family ties, the basic learnings, habits and attitudes of the system are so deeply ingrained in the individual that he looks for a work environment with which he can identify himself; an environment where he finds a kartā-like figure to guide and mould him. It is because of our cumulative experiences and need to hold on to our heritage, that we seek out a symbolic parent figure in the workplace through whom we feel empowered, protected and in whom we can repose our confidence. When we feel this need to relate with others, it releases positive energy like intimacy, togetherness, mutual understanding and respect. Behaviour based on these positive energies and relationship facilitates integration between individual and organizational goals.

Other behavioural reflections and impact of values developed in the joint family system, on the organizational process, are fewer power games and groupism, smoother relationships, higher empathy and camaraderie, acceptance of authority and empowerment.

The kartā style is all encompassing, creating trust and shared values. A true kartā is characterized by an empowering orientation. Empowering and shaping the subordinates through positivity and unconditional acceptance helps in building the subordinate a total person, who thereby learns to take risk and make independent decisions. The superior, in such an environment, shows tolerance to the subordinate's mistakes and converts them into learning experiences. This style genuinely concerns itself emotionally and intellectually with the people and facilitates individual growth through the process of support and advice.

It would therefore be a justified assumption that a management style based on the values of joint family system, under a kartā style leadership, makes for a great business perspective—an indigenous answer to dozens of trial and error management styles that have not been rooted in the Indian context!

Suresh Krishna, chairperson and managing director of Sundaram Fasteners Ltd, who has been successfully practising the paternalistic—kartā—style of management for over three decades, has beautifully summed up:

> Let us not look at what is going around the world, because sometimes it works and sometimes it doesn't. Let us look at ourselves, our values, our ethos, our culture, our joint family systems, what the worker wants; let us find an answer for that and then I am sure, we will be able to mobilize our resources, so that India becomes not only internally competitive but internationally competitive.

Culture and ethos of country is very strongly embedded within any human being who comes to the organization, especially the fact that they come from a very engaged family atmosphere. Over the ages, the family has proved to be the strongest institution and we must try to make use of the strengths of the system and its philosophy. *Ancient wisdom is in perfect balance with the cosmic principles and can be aligned to the corporate world.*

Learnings from the Hofstede's Cultural Dimensions and Indian Culture[73]

Amongst the six dimensions, Indian culture scores highest (77) on power distance. Obedience is the normal expectation, so is employee expectation that they will be told what they are supposed to do. Control is familiar, even a psychological security, and attitude towards managers are formal even if one is on first name basis. Communication is top-down and is essentially directive (see Table 21.1).

The next highest score is on masculinity (56). However, display of masculinity is tempered by societal premium on humility and abstinence.

Uncertainty avoidance score is low (40). People are tolerant of imperfection and the unexpected with the famous 'chalta hai' (it is okay, even if not okay) attitude. People generally do not feel driven and compelled to take action initiatives and comfortably settle into established rolls and routines without questioning. Rules are often in place just to be circumvented and one relies on innovative methods to 'bypass the system'. A word used often is 'adjust', which means a wide range of things, from turning a blind eye to rules being flouted to finding a unique and inventive solution to a seemingly insurmountable problem. It is this attitude that is both the cause of misery as well as the most empowering aspect of the country. There is a saying that 'nothing is impossible' in India so long as one knows how to 'adjust'. This gives rise to entrepreneurial instincts.

India's lowest score is on indulgence (26), leading to a lot of cynicism and pessimism. People feel restrained by social norms.

Amongst other markers, India's intermediate score on individualism shows that it is both a collectivistic and individualistic society. Relationship is based on expectations—Loyalty by the employee and almost familial protection by the employer. The Individualist aspect of Indian society is seen as a result of its dominant religion/philosophy—Hinduism. Dominance of karma and *prarabdh* means that each one is responsible for the results one gets for their actions.

The above is not an exhaustive interpretation of Indian culture's standing on Hofstede dimensions. We also have to keep in mind the changing values and norms with the advent of the millennial generation, to build a culture that is not only attuned to the changing milieu but capitalizes on core strengths of Indian ethos.

Table 21.1. Indian Culture Hofstede Scores and Implications for Change Management

Variable	Score	High/Med/Low	Features	Implications
Power distance	77	High	Acceptance of authority, top-down directive communication	Greater acceptance of fiat
Masculinity/feminism	56	High	Ostentatious display (tempered by value of abstinence and humility)	Create and celebrate small wins in a modest way
Uncertainty avoidance	40	Med–low	Acceptance of imperfection, rule indifference	Regimentation may be counterproductive, if hurried. Promote entrepreneurism
Individualism/collectivism		Medium	Respect for group but individual accountability	Attend to group, as well as One-on-one communication
Indulgence	26	Low	Cynicism and pessimism, restrained by social norms	Focus on culture, social norms
Long-term orientation	51	Medium	Karmic philosophy, patience, low punctuality	Focus on public good and ethics

CHAPTER 22

Values as General Ideals and Standards

Try not to become a man of success but rather try to become a man of value.

—Albert Einstein

Anything and everything we do, either consciously or unconsciously, is based on our beliefs, attitudes and values. *A value is a deeply held belief upon which we act by preference.* The idea of what the right thing to do in a situation comes from our values. It may be termed as a principle which determines our decision for the choice of our action. It is our conception of what is good and desirable, our conviction of what ought to be. Our attitude is an expression of our values.

Karp and Abramms give an interesting analogy:

Think of a value as a lighthouse. A lighthouse maintains a central and clear position of visibility. It does not call all boats into the harbor to anchor there; its function is to direct shipping safely. In other words, a lighthouse's primary function is to direct shipping away from itself and toward the intended destinations. The message is, 'As you go where you are going, keep me in view, or you risk becoming lost.' Values define who you are. Actions get you what you want. When things chronically go wrong for a person at work or at home, it is frequently because of a fundamental inconsistency between that person's value and his actions. The person is behaving in a way that is inconsistent with his own nature.[74]

High values lead to fair and objective decision and action by leaders, ensuring the welfare of all concerned. Values keep a leader on track. We can possess these higher values only through realization that there is a higher dimension guiding and governing the entire human existence.

Where Do Values Come from?

The values we live by are not external in nature. They are neither a manifestation of some kind in our bodies nor something genetically inherited. One might wonder, then, as to the source of these values, which constantly guide us and make us who we are in every way. Why is one individual affable and the other unfriendly? Why is one person on a team so giving and the other extremely self-centred? The judgement about any act being right or wrong is possible only when we have the freedom to choose one or the other and it is here that we need the science of values.

Human values come from our deeper state of being—the consciousness. Our depth dimension is the centre of all values. To most of us, the source of this depth dimension is the existence of the divine force within us. To some, it derives from the 'true north' principles derived from the universal laws of nature. To some others, they are derived from civic consciousness and tenets of peaceful coexistence and mutual growth.

Family and childhood experiences and ongoing occurrence of various events also play an important role in shaping our values. During childhood, our family members, peers, teachers and religious affiliations help us discover our values. Our experiences from school, family rituals, celebrations, styles of interaction—all have an impact on our value formation. As we grow, we experience new feelings, emotions and conflict within ourselves, which create a major impact on our values. As a result of such self-discovery, we see our earlier beliefs in a completely new light. Things altogether change when we undergo this type of advanced learning through internal self-discovery. As we learn more about ourselves, we increase our own self-confidence and perception of self-worth.

The true strength of mankind springs from within. Irrespective of religious and cultural diversities, there exists a remarkable degree of agreement about values, such as humility, truthfulness, forgiveness, selflessness, integrity and gratitude, the richest resources of which are available in the scriptures of all religions of the world, which have guided mankind through the ages.

Organizational Values

J. R. D. Tata once said, 'If someone were to ask me, what holds the Tata companies together, more than anything else, I would say it is our shared ideals and values which we have inherited from Jamshedji Tata.'[75]

Organizational values are shaped by the individual values of leaders, and very often created by the values of the founding fathers. If such values are used as the basic criteria for selecting successors, the organization is bound to flourish.

The group chairperson of Mega Corporation once made certain interesting observations about organizational values:

Values are different for different people, different for different organizations. The collective practice of values is expressed in terms of outcome. I am interested in outcome and cannot trade in individual values and temperaments. Goals are important and also how do we achieve the goals. Tree cannot be separated from the wood and, therefore, it is impossible to have a collective value system. Align everyone to goals and never attempt to align values. Every individual is different in terms of values and instead of aligning their values, align them to organizational goals so that you could achieve them.

However, there was a consensus amongst the business heads and change facilitator on the values of transparency, empathy and so on as the cornerstone of change effort in Mega Corporation. Events have later proved that these contributed in the perception of moral force and mutual trust. This was recognized by the union and the workers and made them open to debate their otherwise entrenched positions.

A management that is satisfied with the routine functions and achievement of physical targets cannot provide the required support for the formation of organizational values. A shared ambition in terms of goal or targets is not enough to create a sense of purpose. It is not enough to define what the company aims to achieve. To create purpose, it is important to shape and embed in the company a set of shared values, which determine the rationale for which an organization exists and provide a description of what kind of company it wants to be.

It is equally, if not more important to know 'who we are' than 'where we are going'. Goals will change as the world around us changes but the core values give an identity to the company, endure as a source of guidance and inspiration and hold the organization together. To hold any organization together, there is a need for an enduring and binding force, which would enable people to be comfortable in taking decisions and forging ahead with planned actions. The core values need to be integrated into every employee-related process—hiring methods, performance management system, promotions, rewards and exit policies. Organizational decisions should be based on these core values alone and once embedded into its systems, the values also need to be promoted at every turn. Since they define meaning for the organization, they should ideally become a constant backdrop against which changing strategies and operating procedures are reliably enacted. It would be justified to state that commitment to ideas, actions, decisions and directions are intense in organizations where a value system is in place.

People can be relied on to do the right things once they buy into and internalize organizational values. As employees internalize them, values can serve as a control system against violations as decisions are taken supported by reference to these. They serve as a guide in cases of controversy or disagreement. These organizational values when discussed with suppliers, distributors and other business partners, demonstrate as to what the company stands for, creating a high image for the company. Statement about organizational values invokes a higher purpose, a purpose beyond current challenges that indicates service to society. This purpose can become a source of competitive differentiation and enhanced brand reputation. These organizations also have fewer problems attracting and retaining talent.

As per Collins and Porras, 'Core values are the essential and enduring tenets of an organization. A small set of timeless guiding principles, core values require no external justification; they have intrinsic value and importance to those inside the organization.' They have also quoted Ralph S. Larsen, CEO of Johnson & Johnson, who said that even though his core values may be his competitive advantage, but he has them because it comes from his inside.[76]

Azim Premji, chairperson of Wipro, one of the world's most successful companies, expresses his commitment to organizational values:

> To meet the challenges of the future we are prepared to change everything about ourselves except our beliefs and values, as they alone guide, govern and bind us together as an organization. It is essential that we consciously internalize our beliefs and be fanatical about consistently practicing them. If we fail to honor our beliefs, we will lose credibility, not only as individuals, but also as an organization. Our beliefs define our basic philosophy of managing business and will remain the spirit and essence of Wipro.[77]

Other such successful and world-class organizations in the country include Infosys, Tata Group and Sundaram Fasteners Ltd, which have deep commitment to their organizational values, and all their strategies are formulated and decisions are taken in the backdrop of these values. These organizations have proved that it is possible to run a business successfully without compromising on values and beliefs. If the head of the organization can establish overarching corporate values, he can get the whole organization working effectively in the same broad direction.

Values initiative should not be treated as a onetime event measured by the initial attention it receives, such as a marketing launch. It is important for a value team to arrive at a statement that works than to reach a decision it may later regret. Leaders and executives should discuss values over a long period; they should consider and reconsider how the standards will play out within their corridors.

In AG Corporation, the vision, mission and values were discussed and debated amongst team of senior executives and later finalized for the company through a two-day workshop attended by the top team and heads of departments. The strategy to institutionalize them was also worked out. It was decided that all executives would repeat them at every chance they get and employees were reminded that organizational values form the basis of every decision the company makes. *Frequent discussions about organizational values can be engaging and empowering. The organization becomes a community united by shared purpose.*

Dr B. M. Munjal, chairperson, Hero MotoCorp, one of India's most successful companies, while talking about organizational values, says:

I have always believed that business should be based on intrinsic values which stand the test of the time. The values, which hold true for life, should hold true for business as well. I have always believed that ethics, along with integrity and character, remain unchanged, in good times or bad times. In fact, I am convinced that the global economic crisis had something to do with violating value-based principles. We call these principles, Dharma.

I am fortunate that my elders imbibed very strong ethical values in me and the lessons that I learnt from them have been my guiding light all these years. These are the teachings of our Vedas, which have been passed on through the ages, and which I believe should form the basis of leadership even today. These include: coping with success and failures with focus on karma; focusing more on the deed and less on the outcome; never forgetting the merits of humility and hard work; doing right things as opposed to doing things right; respecting individuals; and finally, enjoying the journey and not worrying about the destination.[78]

Organizational values are perhaps more important today than at any other time in history because of the fast-changing and dynamic business environment. Who we are as an organization and what we stand for are just as important as what we manufacture or deliver.

CHAPTER 23

Indian Values as Civilizational Backdrop

Yesterday's kings played the same role as today's leaders. As per classical wisdom given in various scriptures, the duties of the king (leader) included protection, growth and development of the state (business entity), sustaining and enhancing the general (stakeholders) welfare, maintaining internal order (organization's culture), and according precedence to public interest (welfare) over his self-interest. This understanding of a 'king' is in the pure classical form, with equanimity and gratitude towards all sectors of society, and not the autocratic image of a glamorous king we associate with fairy tales!

Yajur Veda (9/22) mentions the oath to be administered to the king: 'This kingdom is entrusted to you. You are its director, controller and upholder of this responsibility. This kingdom is given to you for the welfare and prosperity of agriculture and nurture of the subjects.'

As per this oath, the first duty of the king (leader) is to protect his state (organization) and his *praja* (stakeholders) and at the same time enhance their respective welfare. In the happiness of the subject rests the happiness of the king and in what is beneficial to the subject, rests his own benefit.

These leaders of yesterday well understood that morals and values are the cornerstones of society, and this gave them the conviction to rise above temporary provocations. *The basic Indian philosophy looks for congruence between the internal and the external and a synthesis between spoken words and actual behaviour.* The kings used to set an example by living this philosophy and devoting themselves to general welfare.

Indian philosophy is based upon an introspective metaphysics. In their research paper 'Value Identification for Effective Performance' Manoharan and Jayaraman identified seven values from Indian traditions and culture viz. achievement, right conduct, selflessness, sacrifice, emotional detachment, unity in diversity and low priority for accumulating wealth. Indian philosophy emphasizes that work is a *sadhana* or a striving towards the goal of realizing the divinity within us and not simply to satisfy our needs.[79]

Indic philosophy and values are not associated with a particular religion or society. They are called: human values, emanating from *Sanatana Dharma*, the universal religion. According to our scriptures, there are certain common codes, which are applicable to all: truthfulness, non-violence, self-control, purity of mind and body, compassion, equanimity, righteousness, simplicity and so on The two important values in Jain religion are: doing good to others and thinking good of others. Buddhism focuses on the path of holistic living for the good and happiness of many, for compassion, goodness and good things of life to all. The great Indian philosopher, Chanakya, inspired Indian kings to seek success in administration by the method of righteous action, leading to manifestation of divinity within.

Indian ethos always seeks to arouse the 'whole person', the essential divinity and infinite strength within, which ensures success, both internal and external. Based on his study of Buddhist, Vedantic and Yogic psychology, as well as derivative epic and Pauranic literature, S. K. Chakraborty has distilled the values rooted in the deep structure of Indian culture and society and which could be organically more valid and resonant for the Indian psyche in the Indian management context.[80] These values are:

- *The individual must be respected*: Not because of his or her individuality but because of the transcendent, the divine enshrined in him or her, whether good or bad, older or younger, rich or poor.

- *Cooperation and trust*: Because the divine inner being of all individuals is a unity—deception or deprivation of others is deception of deprivation of oneself; besides such inner disposition also helps the digestion, believe it or not.
- *Jealousy is harmful for mental health*: Just as cigarette smoking is harmful for physical health.
- *Chitta-Shuddhi or purification of mind*: With the noble thoughts of compassion, friendliness, humility, gratitude and so on, these *bhavanas* lead to a refined and accurate perception of human relationships, contributing to sounder decisions.
- *Top-quality product/service*: Which is primarily a function of the quality of the mind or consciousness of doer, and only secondarily of quality circles or statistical quality control.
- *Work is worship*: Because the best way to approach the divine through secular life is to offer each piece of work mentally—in as complete, perfect, humble, and pure in form and spirit as one offers a flower or a fruit or a sweet to Him—this can stimulate work ethic in the healthiest way. When work is treated as worship, it leads to excellence in task performance.
- *Containment of greed*: Whether of tangibles (e.g., money) or intangibles (e.g., praise), because it causes stress and robs the individual of wisdom.
- *Ethico-moral soundness*: Because every action or Karma is a cause for a subsequent effect—wholesome as well as unwholesome— and also because ethico-moral soundness gives peace of mind and promotes mental health.
- *Self-discipline and self-restraint*: Because they conserve energy, strengthen will power, create trust and confer dignity.
- *Customer satisfaction*: Because he is the divine come upon us in human garb.
- *Creativity*: Because human creativity is an integral component and extension of cosmic creativity; but this link has to be experientially cultivated through mind stilling.
- *The inspiration to give*: As opposed to the motivation to need, grab and so on because giving is more fulfilling, it adds more meaning to

work and life; also, the individual lives in society with 'debts' to supra-human, human and sub-human beings. Besides, giving with humility is more dignified than petty needs.

- *Renunciation and detachment*: Not of or from duties and responsibilities, but of/from selfish results/rewards and egotistic demands in the workplace; of/from the lower, unregenerate ego and its vanities.

Chakraborty feels that it is a very compact profile of human values, anchored in the transcendent aspect of human existence, which Indian management should immediately begin to understand, explore and implement. He also feels that these values still silently nourish Indian society and culture outside the organized, urbanized, university-stamped and rootless upper crust of our population.

The essence of Indian ethos is that there is commonness, universality among us all. There is the essential oneness of life and at a deeper level of an all-pervading consciousness; everything in the world is interconnected. Every individual is part of a cosmic whole and at the same time is himself a whole, full, complete and autonomous self. It is like the drops of water which make up the ocean, but each drop is complete in itself. This calls for treating everyone with love and affection as if they are us.

'He beholds the self in all beings and equally beholds all beings in the self,' says stanza 29 of chapter VI of The Gita. It says that the perfect person is not merely one who has realized his own divinity, but one who has equally understood and has come to live in an intimate knowledge and experience of the divinity inherent in all creatures without any distinction whatsoever.

Values in the Bhagavad Gita

The Bhagavad Gita was composed against the backdrop of a war, where Arjuna felt that the situation was futile and the fight should be abandoned. Sri Krishna, Arjuna's alter ego, tries to help him surface his self-deception and attempts to bring him back to his own self by getting him in touch with the knowledge of the self. Sri

Krishna did not alter the situation in war preparations; he merely talked to Arjuna, thereby liberating him of his '*dharmsankat (moral dilemma)*'. The purpose of Sri Krishna was to help Arjuna take charge of himself, and therefore, he tried to persuade Arjuna see for himself what was ailing him. Once Arjuna's mind became quiet and calm, he found new courage and confidence. The Gita shows that even a balanced human being is sometimes faced with self-doubt, disorientation and scepticism about his own responsibilities and that these can be managed through the process of acknowledging and deep self-reflection.

> 'I find a solace in the Bhagavad Gita that I miss even in the Sermon on the Mount. When disappointment stares me in the face and all alone I see not one ray of light, I go back to the Bhagavad Gita. I find a verse here and a verse there, and I immediately begin to smile in the midst of overwhelming tragedies—and my life has been full of external tragedies— and if they have left no visible, no indelible scar on me, I owe it all to the teachings of the Bhagavad Gita', says Mahatma Gandhi.

The Gita gives us the true philosophy of life, of action and a set of values, as divine wealth.

Stanza 5 of chapter VI says: 'Let a person lift himself by his own self alone, and let him not allow himself to fall; for self alone is the friend of oneself, and this self is the enemy of oneself.'

This verse also closes the escape route of externalization of responsibility for our failures and asks us to look into our own mismanaged self.

In verse 1–3 of chapter XVI of The Gita, Sri Krishna has given 26 divine attributes, ethical and moral values which make us human and are the means of discovering freedom.

- *Fearlessness:* There are many things we fear, particularly the future; or the fear could be centred on some loss—loss of life, of power, possessions, relationships and so on. Fear is a product of our own state of insecurity or imagined inadequacy. Behind the emotion of fear, there is always a thought, which we are not able to discover due to our ignorance. When we gradually remove the ignorance through spiritual evolution, there is knowledge—there is fearlessness.

- *Purity of mind:* It means cleanliness in our interactions. This cleanliness is possible when we are free from deceit, cheating and falsehood in our thinking and have honest intentions and purity of heart. Inner purity enables us to see purity in everyone and generates love, respect, togetherness and good interpersonal relationships.

- *Commitment to the pursuit of knowledge:* Devotion to knowledge is a positive way to persuade the mind to leave its low temptations. To assimilate our own knowledge, which is very much within ourselves, we have to contemplate with mastery over the senses. A mind, thus awakened to the serene joys of the self, will make us a perfect human being.

- *Giving:* It is a deep-rooted cultural value, born out of the capacity to restrain our instincts of acquisition and replace it with the spirit of sacrifice. Giving what is ours without ego, that is, giving in such a way that the person who receives is happy and does not in any way feel small or obligated, is real giving. Charity develops the capacity to detach ourselves from the wealth we possess and gives us an opportunity to serve.

- *Self-control:* This is control at the level of sense organs and organs of action. To tune the mind to the self, we need a subtle energy, which we can discover within ourselves only when we control our sense excesses. This makes us free, powerful and influential.

- *Sacrifice:* It refers to performing daily rituals such as prayer, which help us control the sense organs and take action that is based on dharma (duty), performed without expectation of reward. Doing what is required to be done for a cause, without selfishness, begets bliss.

- *Self-learning:* Regular studies, coupled with understanding and regular, practice give us an atmosphere wherein we can spiritually grow and have the courage to live in self-control of the sense organs, leading to inner wisdom and capacity for self-exploration to understand the real.

- *Self-austerity:* It is reducing our indulgences in the outside world, taking ups, downs, pleasure and pain as just natural laws, gaining more and more energy within ourselves and applying the new-found energy for the purpose of self-development, blissful living and welfare of others.
- *Straightforwardness:* This refers to alignment between the mind, the word and the action. Crookedness in thought, emotions and general conduct develops in us a split personality. Straightforwardness is selfless but purposeful truthfulness and simplicity.
- *Non-injury:* A hurtful act can be physical, verbal or mental, according to the means used and, thus, there has to be absence of hurt or harmlessness in all our actions. Our motives have to be pure and clean and mind trained to be free of harmful intent or violent feeling in thought, word or deed towards all living beings.
- *Truth:* It is only due to fear of facing certain facts about ourselves that we lie. This makes us weak, creating a self-destructive influence and a split in our personality. One is advised to say not only what is truthful but also what is pleasing and beneficial. Though there must be no deceit or ulterior motive in telling the truth, but it must be cushioned so that it does not hurt, but must always be told. While it is important to say what is pleasant, it should not be at the cost of what is true.
- *Controlling anger:* Anger comes from anguish arising from unfulfilled expectations, hurt ego, criticism and discomfort. All of these are controllable and we should have the capacity to check at the right time, waves of anger as they mount so that we do not manifest anger in our actions and damage others and ourselves.
- *Self-denial:* It is basically the spirit of renunciation, not physically renouncing the world but keeping away feelings of ownership and attachment. This refers to performing action as a thing to be done for the love of inner wisdom and purification, leading to self-development. This involves a feeling of surrender where we operate with the consciousness that the work is in our hands but not necessarily the results.

- *Peacefulness:* There is a sequential order strictly followed in the development of thought. If we are conscious of truth, harming none, keeping an even temper, in a spirit of renunciation, we shall come to experience peace and equanimity even in critical situations. Getting worked up detracts us from efficiency while a peaceful mind can successfully keep our inward balance and intellectual poise even in the midst of outrageous circumstances. Peace is resolution of the mind and is possible only if there is no self-judgement. If we stop making judgement on the basis of our mind and learn to accept the facts, we find there is peace.

- *Refrain from criticism:* We normally criticize others because we are not happy within ourselves. Such behaviour is ordered by the personality behind it and is often a way of trying to handle jealousy. Criticism deprives us of the opportunity for self-correction, since, instead of improving ourselves, we try to cover up our own failures and resort to fault-finding in others. We should develop such an inward harmony that our speech should echo the fragrance of sincerity, devotion and love, and we should stay with ourselves to look at the problem that is creating pressure for us to talk about someone else.

- *Compassion:* It is an expression of love towards another being who is in pain of any kind. Our acting upon in such a situation is the expression of love resulting from empathy with the pain of another. It is helping others without their asking for it—it is caring. Compassion is the feeling of tenderness towards all kinds of living beings and love alone can discover an infinite amount of tenderness in us to sweeten our lives. Love is a consciousness, not just an intense feeling for one person or object or a passion. Since love flows from truth, it is selfless as well as self-fulfilling.

- *Absence of ardent longing:* It is about the inherent power in all of us to appreciate objects and sense enjoyment, without a longing arising in us. Even if a fancy occurs, we do not respond to it by way of controlling our sense organs from extreme indulgence. We do our worldly duty without greed or attachment to either physical comforts or money, remaining in self-control without endless hunger amounting to greed.

- *Softness:* If we have established ourselves in the noble qualities, we shall be able to bring forth beauty and harmony in our interface with the world outside. Our behaviour will be gentle and soft and people shall be able to talk to us freely, happily and without fear. Softness implies accommodation, accepting other's limitations and understanding its source.
- *Modesty:* This is particular kind of shyness—shying away from praise and from extolling our own glories—remaining objective and not flattering oneself. Modesty retains harmony of the social fabric around us while excessive unconventionalism discomforts.
- *Freedom from restlessness:* Restlessness of our mind gets reflected in our physical movements, the body shadowing the condition of the mind. A constant restlessness or a sudden outburst of activity or immodest shaking of body are the expressions of agitation in our mind. We need to cultivate a steady character and a purposeful personality through the knowledge of and mastery over self.
- *Energy:* This is not the mere physical glow or shine of our skin but refers to inner brilliance. It is the capacity to face challenges with confidence, and the ability to change and influence the thinking of others. We can serve all and discover a sense of fulfilment through the vigour, spiritedness and abundant energy, achieved by the brilliance of our intellect, the serene poise in our activities, and the expression of love for all, emerging from the innermost depths of our being.
- *Forgiveness:* It is the capacity to face the most powerful opposition and provoking situation with an unruffled serenity. It is composure where there is no change within us even when we are put to physical or mental inconvenience or when insulted or injured by others. In such a situation, anger does not arise and we get an opportunity to understand the other person. Unless we have the readiness to accommodate and allow the person to behave as he is, there is no way of understanding him.
- *Fortitude:* This is the will to survive adversity and sustain our good qualities when the circumstances are unfavourable and the body and sense organs are tired or in pain. The attitude

to stick to our guns and not mind the pain is fortitude. The sacred energy from which fortitude trickles down comes from strength of faith, conviction in the goal, consistency of purpose, vivid perception of the ideal and a bold spirit of sacrifice. This sacred energy gives us the capacity to happily put up with pain and unfavourable circumstances.

- *Purity:* This refers to both the inner and outer cleanliness and purity. External cleanliness and purity of environment is also an important discipline, as it helps create a healthy frame of mind. Inner cleanliness is a mental disposition involving purity of thoughts and motives and is the opposite of one assailed by emotions such as hatred. We have to look into our own mind and as the emotions of hatred, enmity, deceit, likes or dislikes arise, we have to create the opposite attitude and develop a mind that is predominantly pure.
- *Non-hatred:* This includes not only absence of hurting or harming but also absence of even a thought of hurting another. Just as we will never have any idea of injuring ourselves, we, in our recognition of the oneness in all living creatures, must come to feel that to injure anyone is to injure ourselves.
- *Absence of pride:* While a certain amount of self-respect is necessary, demanding respect from others is what is negated here. Working without hankering for fame or recognition is true work. It is about renouncing our over-exaggerated pride and notion of self-honour.

To assure ourselves of a right way of living, we must respect and live these 26 values of life. There is commonness, a universality, among us all. Treating everyone with affection, love and concern, as if they are our own selves, is the true path to freedom and perfection—a true path to good leadership too.

One of the most successful change efforts in modern Indian history was freedom movement, piloted by Mahatma Gandhi. One can checklist most of the values enumerated above. They were also reflected in his simplicity of attire, his cordiality with his opponents, authenticity and so on.

PART VII

INDIAN MODEL FOR DRIVING CHANGE

So far, in this book, we have looked at the following:

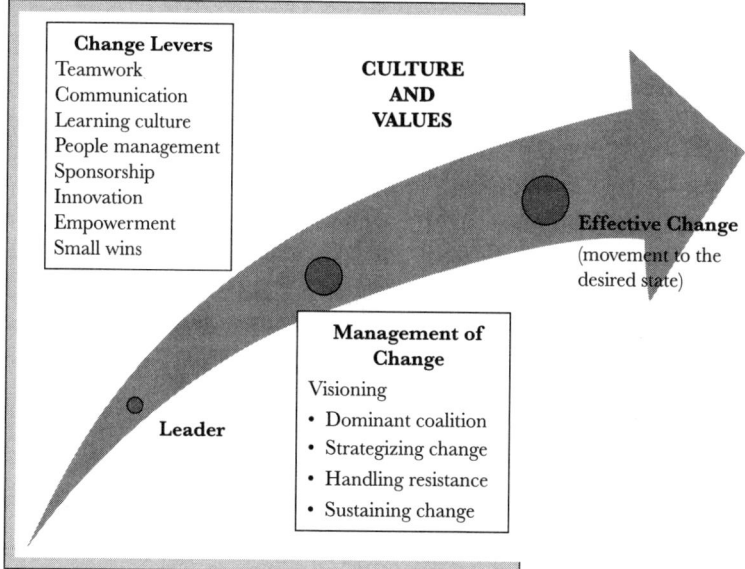

The importance of culture and values has been emphasized and deliberated in detail. However, despite similarity in management practices and technology across the world, there are distinct management cultures in American, German, Chinese and Japanese organizations. These distinctions often influence how people will relate to each other, how change will be effected and so on. There are significant cultural overlays influencing the effectiveness and success of change efforts. This is understood widely and that is why multi-country expat experience is a necessary component in grooming of global leaders. This is especially important in a country like India where roots of some of these underpinnings of culture go back to several millennia.

Therefore, change management is not a matter of simply following a particular model or following steps. If change always followed an exact pattern, if it was always predictable, there would not be any need for different models. The right approach will be specific to the situation and organization culture. We need to customize our change efforts based on the unique characteristics of the change in question, the attributes of the organization and the cultural ethos of the society it belongs to.

Models of change are useful in that they describe and simplify a process and enable an understanding of the connection between the elements involved, but copying something foreign, though more glamorous and alluring, is not wisdom, as that disturbs the inner psychological composure in the long run, especially coming from a society whose values are different.

Warren Bennis, one of the most perceptive and experienced writers on leadership, a distinguished professor at Southern California University and adviser to four US Presidents, writes about the decline of American society and its industrial environment.

> The new corporate thinking casts CEOs as global warriors rather than national ones. In other words, nothing counts except profits, and profits count because they are the sole measure of the CEO. Conscience and competence take a backseat to ambition, as the wheel that turns the fastest gets the bonus. There was a time when CEOs were civic leaders and corporate statesmen. Today, they have no interest in anything but their own bottom lines. The visionaries, too, are gone. Only sure-fire products and systems win the attention of the CEO, who has neither the time nor the inclination to commit his or her company to a potentially innovative or even useful product. Our best qualities are integrity, dedication, magnanimity, humility, openness, and creativity. These, of course, are the basic ingredients of leadership, and our unwillingness to tap these qualities in ourselves explains, to a large extent, the leadership shortage.[81]

Systems and practices are developed keeping in mind the social, political, economic and cultural needs of the society, and what we are doing is trying to copy the systems of a society, which itself is unhealthy, a society which practices individualism and self-interest and where the law is treated as an instrument of assault. Indian organizations are struggling to implement these frameworks effectively because they are still not aligned to the Indian culture and environment. The Indian model for managing change has to be developed based on the Indian context of societal norms, culture, economic and socio-political factors, as well as value system of the people. Leading change is about leading people as whole as they are.

The people in the East have a different orientation; they are taught the meaning of life and raised on the teachings of scriptures, saints and philosophers such as Chanakya, Confucius and Lao-Tzu. They are taught to concentrate all their energies on actions and not always clinging to expectations about the fruits of their labour. Indian philosophy balances the pursuit of wealth and material success with the mastery of the self and the quest for inner happiness.

In his very thought-provoking article 'Theorizations on Leadership', T. V. Rao says that there is plenty of theory on leadership —much of it from the West, a bit from the East and a little from India itself.[82] Based on the study of these theories, he has given a few trends of leadership but has also mentioned that the trends so analysed give rise to many questions for which the practitioners should provide answers. The key question is what are the characteristics needed of leaders today given the realities of our culture and stage at which we are in our organizations? What qualities help a CEO or top manager lead his organization and make an impact?

While mentioning that much of the leadership theory is from the West, Rao has posed an important question of what are the characteristics needed of leaders today given the realities of our culture, where he also talks about the Indian mind, referring to our value system.

Arnold Toynbee, Nobel laureate, while lauding Indian ethos and wisdom, says:

> It is already becoming clear that a chapter which had a western beginning in business management will have to have an Indian ending, when the world adopts rich thoughts of Indian ethos and wisdom, if it is not to end in the self-destruction of the human race.[83]

What are other cultural overlays in Indian context? A millennia-old culture may not be visible at first sight but continues to influence Indian mind in myriad ways, especially in the context of change. An Indian mind looks around for moorings in values embedded in its conscious and sub-conscious mind. Awareness of these influences has helped up propose the following model for change.

To begin with, just as Dharma is context- and time-specific, as opposed to absolutist concept of religion, this model acknowledges that the appropriate model to be adopted in any given context will have to be arrived after taking into consideration *Paristhiti* (socio-political-cultural environment) and *Manyatāyen* (local values) along with *Parikalpana* (vision and growth ambitions).

Indian Model of Change Management

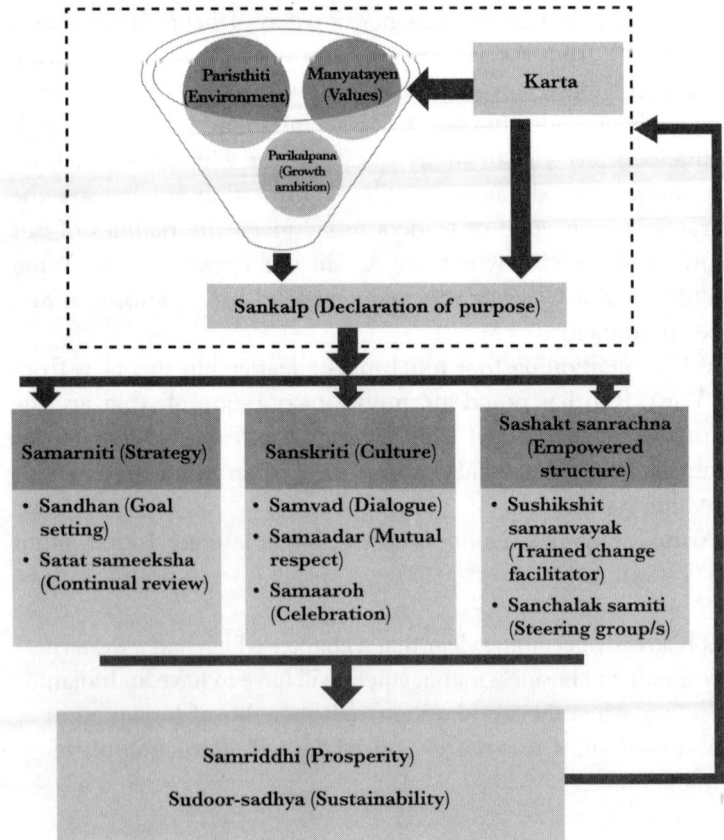

Sankalp

Of these, values are the most distinctive part. If these values are in accordance with Indian ethos and culture, change management creates less resistance and has greater chances of success. We have already discussed the distinctiveness of Indian values in the minds of a majority of Indian entrepreneurs and industrialists. At the risk of repetition, some of the common ones are premium on karma as the final arbiter (as in *karmayog*), seeing organization as an extended/ joint family, restraint in conduct, respect for nature, welfare for the masses (even those not a direct part of the organization, as evident in construction of health and education facilities and so on). These values guide the world view, including how changes are perceived in the environment and how to adapt self and the organization from the long-term objective of Samriddhi (prosperity) and Sthāyitva (sustainability). One of the necessary functions of a leader is to have a Parikalpanā (vision).

So these values of top leadership play a part at three levels. First, choice of growth direction. Second, choice of technology and its impact on present employment. Many Indian business houses hesitate in adopting technologies that would drastically reduce employment. Third, choice of strategies businesses would adopt on how to bring about change.

All these inputs combine to create not only a compelling need for change but also broad contours of the way forward.

As mentioned earlier, particularly in Mega Corporation, a full-fledged cell was created comprising professionals with not only domain knowledge of people management and IRs but also industrial engineers, planners, statisticians and so on, who rendered invaluable help in data collection on environmental challenges, industry-wide productivity statistics, best practices and so on. These data were useful not only for creating and promoting a compelling need for change but also for sharing these with various employee groups, including worker representatives, including for creating a supportive climate for change.

Karta Leadership

The organization being an extended family, we need a philosophy of leadership that is always focused on enlisting the hearts and minds of the members through inclusion and participation. Winning over hearts and minds and dealing with emotional aspect of change is a difficult and draining task. When we talk of changing mindsets or mental models, we try to persuade the individuals to give up some of his assumptions and beliefs. This can take place only by way of influencing and persuasion, which people will accept only if it comes from someone whom they trust, respect and who has credibility. Even if people do not completely agree with the proposed change, they are more likely to go along with it, as they tend to have confidence in those they trust. We need leaders with wisdom and understanding of cultural ethos to cope with the emotions of people. We need Kartā like leader to manage this larger family in the manner s/he manages the joint family. Kartā is epitomized as an empowered and empowering, omnipresent, guiding, protecting and caregiving entity in the collective (joint family). Thus, kartā becomes the anchor. However, following the value system, she or he does not impose but inspires individuals and encourages them to move forward based on this intrinsic motivation. Hence, she or he is not a hierarchical position. In an interview with the author, Dr Harismita Trivedi says:

> Indian ethos slightly defers from the western concept of 'power distance'—in that it is less about hierarchy and more about respect, a fulfilment of the need for security and care. 'Power' here is that of 'expert' power. Western interpretation of 'power' in this context is essentially 'position' power.

The kartā extends warmth, affection, care and nurturance to everyone in the family, has empowering orientation, and guides the direction of individual growth and development through support, advice, training and counselling. She or he is demanding, affectionate, listens to everybody in the family, gives importance to everybody, takes care of their interests, is easily approachable, consults others and takes decisions keeping in mind the welfare of the family as his or her sole concern. Warmth and other traits as possessed by kartā-like leader are the conduit of influence that facilitate trust, communication and absorption of ideas.

It is to be noted that kartā is a role prototype that is performed by the head of the organization, independent of whether it is a family-run or professionally managed organization. Chief characteristics and benefits of kartā leadership are summarized below:

- Operates from a strong sense of values of compassion, fairness and nurturance.
- Is always sensitive to the feelings of others.
- Can effectively deal with emotional side of change.
- Releases positive energy such as intimacy, togetherness, mutual understanding and respect. This, in turn, facilitates integration between individual and organizational goals.
- With a kartā-like figure, people trust him or her and look for emotional support in formal work environment.
- With high level of trust and credibility in the leader, the communication becomes effective and ideas get easily absorbed.
- Persuasion and influencing by a person with high level of trust and credibility helps in creating willingness for and commitment to change.
- It becomes easier to bring change in mental models, mindsets and behaviour.
- Employees feel empowered and protected.
- Basic human factors are taken care of.

What is distinctive in a kartā leader vis-à-vis other models of leadership? With the possible exception of an odd person with a violent childhood from broken homes, the word 'family' invokes nostalgia of a nurturant leadership, the one that supported, developed and took care of one's needs within the overall constraints of fairness and budget. A kartā leader is supposed to take care of the members of the organization as a family elder. In traditional Indian organizations, it is not unusual for the owner to go out of the way for taking care of medical, educational or financial needs of a wedding in the family of a worker even at the lowliest echelon. This is just one of the many ways the owner may promote the concept of an organization as an extended family. Overall amount spent this way in a year may not be very high, but the owner gets rewarded with a life-long loyalty of most members of the organization. In such organizations, many people even forego growth and progression during periods of difficulty and change. Of course, younger employees, including the millennials, may no longer be as enamoured of the family concept as some of the older generations. Yet, kartā-type leadership remains a potent element of Indian model of change management due to its inherent positivity and management based on trust.

Contrary to the perceptions of some, 'kartā' leadership is gender neutral. In many business families, it is the matriarch who holds the sway and performs the same functions as the patriarch in some other families. There are misconceptions that our cultural ethos supports patriarchy. In a culture where there are more female deities than male ones, where rise of Durga to take on demons when everyone else failed is celebrated, acceptance of female leaders is more natural than widely believed.

Similarly, it is not always even single person. For example, in Patanjali group, this function is being performed by two persons, Ramdev and Balkrishna.

Samarniti

One of the key roles of kartā in the management of change is to guide, assist and support in the development of *Sahmati* (consensus) for chalking out strategies, goals and plan of action *(Sandhān)* for bringing about change. It is NOT an imposing role. In a survey of top Indian leaders on what their key responsibilities are, Capelli et al.[84] listed chief input for organizational strategy and keeper of organizational culture as the top two and representation of owner and investor interests as the fourth priority, whereas looking after owner and investor interests was the topmost priority of Western leaders.

Satat Sameeksha (continual review) ensures that the strategy, structure (and processes) and culture are in alignment considering emergent situations both inside and outside the organization. This also includes continual review to keep systems and processes simple because there is an inherent tendency for increasing complexity in an attempt for greater responsiveness to fast-changing world. The challenge here is also to address the paradox of increasing personal autonomy while keeping in check functional autonomy by institutionalizing capability development a multifunctional/business unit-wide endeavour. Progressive induction of digitalization, analytics and widely shared metrics aligned to organizational goals helps keep everyone on the same page in a transparent manner. There are organizations where these metrics are not only used to assess organizational performance but also each unit's/department's performance.

Sashakt Sanrachna

The most critical responsibility of kartā, especially in middle or large-sized organizations, is to:

- Appoint a *Sushikshit Samanvayak* (change facilitator or a coordinator) and *Sanchālak Samiti* (steering group). It is essential that the change facilitator should be trained and competent. Alternatively, he should be trained in change management and project management skills.
- Assign clear responsibilities to each strategic role, while at the same time, encouraging collaborative focus on results.
- Disseminate information about these appointments and their roles and responsibilities.
- Reinforce their charter through unambiguous public support and appropriate empowerment.

Chief facilitator may be the convener of the key steering group. This role has two types of eligibility and suitability. She or he should preferably be well versed in change/project management practices. More importantly, she or he should be strong in communication, people skills and resilience. Prosci's recommendations on this topic has been discussed earlier in the book.

Steering group usually comprises all or most of the key role holders/influencers in areas/functions where change management is proposed, along with support functions. In multi-location large organizations, there may be location-wise facilitators and steering groups.

We have seen the utility of these roles in the change efforts discussed earlier in the book. We have also talked about earlier the unusually substantial amount of time to build cohesion, transparency and collective responsibility towards the success of change efforts, especially in Mega Corporation.

In small organizations, challenge of change management is not so massive. Therefore, the kartā herself/himself may mantle the role of the coordinator and assemble a team of function heads as a steering group.

It is also important to note that in this digital age, change is fast becoming a continual, if not continuous activity more than major discrete changes. In such a situation, major part of change management responsibility may rest with one person formally designated for the purpose with IT/HR function providing the bulk of support.

Sanskriti

Sandhān

Once the need articulation and determination to embark on the journey of change has been taken, the next step is to set final and intermediate goals. As mentioned earlier, it is very critical to set short-term and intermediate goals so that those involved and those affected by change continue to experience and celebrate successes amidst pain of change. This can make all the difference between success and failure, especially as the journey may take months and years.

To appreciate the criticality of the middle, it is worthwhile to note what Rosabeth Moss Kanter says, 'Welcome to the miserable middles of change. This is the time when Kanter's Law kicks in. Everything looks like a failure in the middle. Everyone loves inspiring beginnings and happy endings; it is just the middles that involves hard work'[85] and she gives an example of gooey sticky mess in the middle in the transition from caterpillar to butterfly. This middle period is the most frustrating when people begin to experience the costs of change, including attritions, missing friends and colleagues, increased workloads, and start doubting the utility of the whole exercise.

It is here that mid-term successes act as booster shots in the middle.

Samvād and Samādar

The next most essential ingredient in the process of change is creating an organization-wide *Samvād (dialogue)* and arousing emotional energy about the need for change and the desire to participate. We normally underestimate the enormity of this task of awakening. *Samvād* is not communication even though communication is part of *Samvād*. Additionally, *Samvād* underscores the validity and *Samādar* (mutual respect) for counterviews and the need for developing a broad consensus, a shared vision for change. Managers and senior leaders have to play the key role in promoting acceptance and developing support for change. Gaining commitment to a new direction is not an easy task and calls for a well-planned strategy. It is the most powerful force bringing everyone closer to seeing the truth and understanding the whole picture to capture the hearts and mind of employees. Repeated and well-planned communication is the first step and, understandably, *Samādar* for everyone can be frustrating if there is a divergence, but we must not forget that change happens only through people; therefore, management of change is not only rational management but also emotional management of people. In this context, Samvād and Samādar help in managing emotional effects of change, dissipating any negative energy. Thus, they help in creating an ownership for change, a feeling that 'we' wanted the change, instead of just the management.

This Samvād has to be at four levels: from kartā and dominant coalition/change facilitator to the entire organization and influencers, from first-line supervisors to rank-and-file employees, from influencers to people under influence, and from kartā and other external interface officials to other stakeholder groups, including media and government agencies. The last is important, particularly in case of major change and where other entities are involved, for example, in case of acquisitions and mergers.

> Not only *Samvād*, but continuous dialogue (*Satat Samvād*) and mutual respect at all levels and stages were a critical lever of change in both the successful change programmes discussed in the book.

Samāroh

Launch is equally important; a *puja* or *anushthaan* or just a plain celebration, seeking divine blessings infuses the whole project with certain amount of sanctity, something important in Indic consciousness, even among atheists. Act of seeking divine blessings need not be restricted to any particular religion; it can even be couched in secular terms. Celebration is a significant part of the strategy for the emotional alignment of people. These celebrations can be held at each milestone of change project. *Samaaroh* is also a thanksgiving—a celebration that acknowledges the support of the divine.

> We have already mentioned in earlier chapters that initiation of *havan* and involvement of people's representatives in this endeavour was an important part of the overall strategy in Mega Corporation.

Shubh Lābh

This is a standard phrase written on the walls and account books of most businesses in India, as part of the local tradition. One wonders if the meaning (i.e., auspicious profits) is equally widely understood. Auspicious profits could mean one or more of the three things:

1. The fervent hope of the presence of divine blessing: That is why, in traditional businesses, it is often accompanied by images of Ganesha (the deity responsible for removal of irritants and bottlenecks) and Lakshmi (the deity of wealth) or Swastika (symbolizing good luck or divinity). In every Asian/oriental culture, there are such symbols which denote divine blessings.
2. It has been obtained in production/trading of goods and services *through ethical means*/value-based leadership.
3. The cause itself is noble, for example, hospitals and pharmaceuticals, education and so on. Our purpose of including this in Indian change model is that it imbues the change effort with a certain positivity, legitimacy and sanctity in the minds of the masses, aiding (though not guaranteeing) acceptance and compliance. This is reinforced through *Samārohs*.

Incidentally, there is no rejection of this phrase even by the secular-minded because of cultural context, even though they may not buy into the symbolism.

Change inevitably involves pain and sacrifices at least in the short and medium term for a significant section of employees, if not all employees. Engaged employees are willing to bear a lot more pain than disengaged employees. What triggers disengagement? One is the absence, or inadequacy of three pillars of engagement—mastery, autonomy and significance/purpose. Second is the perception of breach of psychological contract by the management. Third is the perception that the company may not be following ethical practices in its operations.

If the company is perceived by the employees to be following ethical practices and/or is engaged in the business that has a significant positive impact on the community/society at large; this goodwill capital facilitates the implementation of change through deployment of voluntary extra effort by engaged employees. This voluntary extra effort is very valuable because every change involves overload not only by the people who are entrusted with the task of change management in addition to regular duties but also by other employees affected by the change, especially in the transition period.

Both in Mega Corporation and AG Corporation, the above model brought change. After creating organization-wide awareness about the need for change, a well-thought-out strategy was formulated, which was implemented under a *kartā* leadership. Union's General Secretary of Mega Corporation, commenting on the entire process of change, told that though the decisions of the management were tough and firm, there was no ill will against anybody and it did not show any bitter feeling even against those who were negative. The management had no revengeful attitude and showed patience, tolerance and forbearance. Many others also highlighted that the management neither had any hidden agenda nor followed the divide and rule policy and maintained cordial relations even with adversaries. People developed respect for the management's value-based behaviour when it turned down offer of few leaders of calling off strike against money deal as opposed to signing the settlement. The management did not promote any particular group and tried to talk and convince everybody about the need for a change.

The cases in the beginning of the book clearly establish that an unproductive culture can be successfully changed with value-based interventions and that the above model is a tested product. Both these organizations displayed a significant positive change not only in performance in statistical terms but also in terms of attitudes and mindset.

In the words of group chairman of Mega Corporation: 'The proof of having brought the change is that today I do not have anybody resisting change.' While describing the post-change environment, he further said, 'Change keeps spirit, venture, challenge, and breathes enterprise. All this is happening and what I see is that an excellent job has been done.'

Describing the new environment after the change, the Group Chairman observed, 'Today my organization has become flexible from rigid. I am as young as I was yesterday. My yesterday has become my tomorrow.'

Change Facilitator in Chanakya Role

Quite often, HR/IT leaders may complain that the top management/karta does not appreciate the need of major change as a necessity for continued survival and growth. While top management will have to provide the final impetus and support for major change effort, umpteen examples exist where HR/IT leaders have built support coalition and trigger debates that finally led to the initiation of major change. For considerations of avoiding power play, this role may be discrete without attracting undue attention as the driving force, but this will assume more significance in the digital era. In many such cases, combination of HR and IT leaders will be quite potent in providing leadership in helping organizations renew themselves.

Epilogue

The proposed model in the last chapter encapsulates our learning from not only the three cases given in Part II 'Experiences of Change' but also myriad change experiences, big and small, in organizations from the private sector, public sector and multinational corporations, as well as from the accumulated wisdom of thinkers, researchers and practitioners from all over the world. Hence, it is not revolutionary; it merely attempts to incorporate all aspects of change management, besides incorporating cultural thought, nuances and practices that may resonate more with Indian/Asian psyche.

To recap, we summarize the distinctions of the proposed model as follows:

1. Articulate and continually communicate the reason for change and vision.
2. Provide strong, decisive but consensus-seeking leadership keeping in mind the interests of all stakeholders, not merely the owners. Prosperity for all and sustainability is the ultimate goal.
3. Provide empowered structure, including the steering group and the change facilitator. Changed facilitator should be well trained with change management and project management skills. As discussed in the previous chapter and below, in this digital age, some of these responsibilities may regularly rest with one person suitably trained for the purpose. In such a scenario, the required training will become a part of requirement with him or her with bulk support provided by IT/HR.
4. Maintain continuous dialogue with all sections, including influencers and the rank and file, based on mutual respect.
5. Seek divine blessings to give the change effort an image of a sacred endeavour.
6. Set up small wins and celebrate along the way.

We have called it an Indian model for change for distinction as compared to Western approaches, but it is equally applicable in most South Asian and East Asian contexts due to overarching similarity of Eastern thought processes, perhaps because of the imprint of Indic thought across these territories through Hindu and Buddhist influences. Of course, terminologies may differ because of language diversity. There may also be subtle differences in each situation, even though underpinnings may be common throughout the world.

Management of change is more an art than science. Hence, skill of planning and execution along with empathy, communication and compassion without losing the objective will play a greater role in its success. Jim Dornan gives an interesting analogy of shunting in a railway yard. He says that an engine cannot go to the parallel track and ask the coaches to run along and join it. It has to go to the same track on which other coaches are, approach them from the front slowly, hook them and then carry them along. Likewise, in any change effort, the way we approach people to be a part of the change process plays a crucial role. Change management is a hands-on job where one has to be with 'the troops'; It cannot be done through fiats.

Added to this, with progressive use of outsourcing of non-core functions and rapid emergence of gig economy, change management will become a core area for HR function. As we saw in Microsoft and others, change management training and certification as a step to build an in-house pool of change professionals will become common, especially in large organizations. Will AI assist change management too? Possibly yes, especially in mapping employee emotions, particularly when they are operating from diverse locations, including homes, hotels and business centres/co-working spaces, besides regular office campuses.

It will be a cliché to say that the pace of change has not only become unprecedented, but is constantly spiralling exponentially. Organizations will have to continually reinvent themselves to sustain and grow. Therefore, change management may no longer be a discrete project. If it is a discrete project, there may be several such discrete projects running concurrently. We have already discussed in Chapter 3, how the onward march of technology like AI, analytics, machine learning and so on will significantly reduce human involvement in routine and transactional HR functions. By the way, Google CEO Sundar Pichai recently said in MSNBC interview that AI is more profound than fire and electricity in terms of its impact on humanity.

Going further ahead, AI may also help in eliciting shop-floor collaboration and coordination when an increasing number of humans will be replaced by robots/humanoids, and both humans and humanoids will work shoulder to shoulder. This is no space age fantasy; such a scenario is just around the corner. Added to this, organizations will be caught up in swirling tide of mergers, acquisitions and amalgamations. We are also seeing big organizations, such as Satyam, RCOM, Bhushan Steel, ILFC, Jet Airways and so on, falling by the wayside, especially as the Bankruptcy Code becomes more streamlined. In all this, change management will become more and more complex and critical.

Change Management in the Digital Age

Change management itself will undergo transformation in the new era in the following ways, well elucidated by Emma Cullen[86]:

1. Organizations are on a continuous treadmill. Change management will more often be a continuous process than discrete projects. Therefore, there will be all the more necessity to build this as an in-house capacity, probably merged into HR function rather than depending on the change management consultants.

2. Management roles will not be restricted to those with the most experience. As major decisions will become data driven, data science experts will get a seat at the decision-making table irrespective of age. Having said that, data will never be able to accurately predict human behaviour all the time. That will not replace people skills and wisdom to deal with human emotions.

Orbit Change

This phrase was recently discussed by S. K. Sharma[87]—co-founder, ISPIRT Foundation—in SHRM Conference, May 2019. He says that orbit change or shift is that kind of change where an industry changes beyond recognition in 7 to 10 years. He contrasts electricity generation and distribution with telephony. He says that if Edison and Graham Bell were to visit India, Edison will be able to recognize his invention, whereas Bell will not be able to recognize his invention. A similar orbit shift is happening in fintech and banking. In fact, as he says, no one knows what changes are going to happen in the banking industry in the next five years. Similar shifts can be around the corner in other industries as well, such as health care. In fact, Sharma further goes on to prognose that industries in orbit shift will have a larger number of companies on the path of survival and growth than other industries. One can imagine the challenges of change management in such a scenario.

So there are fascinating, challenging and unprecedented times ahead. Let us fasten our seatbelts and let us be ready for exhilarating change!

References

1   Argyris C. (1997). *Overcoming Organizational Defences*. New York, NY: Prentice Hall.
2   Webber A. (May 1999). Learning For a Change. *Fast Company*, 24:178.
3   Nilakant V. & Ramnarayan S. (2006). *Change Management: Altering Mindsets in a Global Context*. New Delhi: SAGE Publications.
4   Morris T. (2002). Speech in European Roundtable Conference. Brussels.
5   Drucker P. F. & Flaherty J. E. (1999). *Shaping Managerial Mind*. San Francisco, CA: Jossey-Bass.
6   Nadler D. A., Shaw R. B., Walton A. Elise & Associates (1994). *Discontinuous Change*. San Francisco, CA: Jossey-Bass.
7   Change Management in Tata Motors (2009). http://eravandi. blogspot.com/2009/12/change-management-in-tata-motors.html (accessed on 6 October 2019).
8   Nilakant V. & Ramnarayan S. (1998). *Managing Organizational Change*. New Delhi: Response Books.
9   Tichy N. M. & Devanna M. (1986). *The Transformational Leader*. New York, NY: John Wiley & Sons.
10 Kotter J. P. (1996). *Leading Change*. Boston, MA: Harvard Business School Press.
11 Beer M., Eisenstap R. A. & Spector B. (1990). Why Change Programmes Don't Produce Change. *Harvard Business Review*, (November–December):158–166.
12 Change Management. www.prosci.com.
13 Brown Brené (2018). *The Power of Vulnerability*. Amazon Audiobooks.
14 Welch J. (1994). *Control Your Destiny or Someone Else Will*. New York, NY: Harper Collins.
15 Vivekananda (1907). *Complete Works of Swami Vivekanada*. Calcutta: Advaita Ashram.
16 Pettigrew A. & Whipp R. (1991). *Managing Change for Competitive Success*. New York, NY: John Wiley & Sons.
17 Lucas J. R. (1998). Anatomy of Vision Statement. *Management Review*, 87(2):22–26.

18 Kotter J. P. (1995). *Leading Change: Why Transformation Efforts Fail.* Boston, MA: Harvard Business School.
19 Balachandran R. (2017). 5 Ways for Effective Team Visioning and Leadership. *SHRM South Asia Blog,* March.
20 Boyett J. H. & Boyett J. T. (1998). Seven Tips for Managing Organizational Change. www.jboyett.com.
21 Prahalad C. K. (1997). Strategies for Growth. *Chairman,* February 28, 3–8.
22 Wang D. (2016). 8 Strategies for Change Management That Actually Work. *Tinypulse,* April.
23 Beshears J. & Gino F. (2014). Experiment with Organizational Change Before Going All In. *Harvard Business Review,* October.
24 Kotter J. P. & Schlesinger L. A. (1979). Choosing Strategies for Change. *Harvard Business Review,* (March–April):106–114.
25 Otala M. (1996). Understanding and Managing Change. *Journal of Organizational Change Management,* 9(6):54–80.
26 Hari Gopal K. (2001). *Management of Organizational Change: Leveraging Transformation.* New Delhi: Response Books.
27 Russell J. & Russell L. (2006). *Leading Change Training.* London: Pergamon Flexible Learning.
28 Morris K. F. & Raben C. S. (1995). *The Fundamentals of Change Management, in Discontinuous Change.* San Francisco, CA: Jossey-Bass.
29 Sirkin H. L., Keenan P. & Jackson A. (2005). The Hard Side of Change Management. *Harvard Business Review,* October. https://hbr.org/2005/10/the-hard-side-of-change-management (accessed on 17 October 2019).
30 Wakhlu A. (1999). *Managing from Heart.* New Delhi: Response Books.
31 Senge P. (1994). *The Fifth Discipline: The Art and Practice of Learning Organization.* New York, NY: Currency Doubleday.
32 Ulrich D. (1997). *Human Resource Champions.* Boston, MA: Harvard Business School Press.
33 Jack W. (2012). The Exit Interview by Rick Kirkland and Geoffrey Colvin. www.Fortune.com.
34 Duck J. D. (1998). *Managing Change: The Art of Balancing, Harvard Business Review on Change.* Boston, MA: Harvard Business School Press.
35 Champy J. A. (1997). Preparing for Organizational Change. In *Organization of the Future.* The Peter F. Drucker Foundation. San Francisco, CA: Jossey-Bass.
36 Larkin T. J. & Larkin S. (1996). Reaching and Changing Frontline Employees. *Harvard Business Review,* May–June. https://hbr.

org/1996/05/reaching-and-changing-frontline-employees (accessed on 17 October 2019).

37 Leonard D. & Coltea C. (2013). Most Change Initiatives Fail—But They Don't Have To. *Gallup Business Journal*, May. https://news. gallup.com/businessjournal/162707/change-initiatives-fail-don.aspx (accessed on 17 October 2019).

38 Toffler A. (1984). *Future Shock*. New York, NY: Bantam Doubleday Dell Publishing.

39 Rao T. V. (1993). Management of Learning in Organizations: Some Reflections. *Personnel Today*, July–September.

40 Huber (1991). Quoted from Yogesh Malhotra's article 'Current Business Concerns and Knowledge Management' on brint.com.

41 Senge P. (1990). The Leader's New Work: Building Learning Organizations. *Sloan Management Review*, Fall. https://sloanreview.mit. edu/article/the-leaders-new-work-building-learning-organizations/ (accessed on 17 October 2019).

42 Gates B. (1999). *Business @ Speed of Thought*. New York, NY: Penguin Books.

43 Narayanamurthy N. R. (2013). Innovation Is Key to Fight Protectionism. *Economic Times*, September. https://economictimes. indiatimes.com/opinion/interviews/innovation-is-key-to-fight-protectionism-narayana-murthy/articleshow/6546117.cms (accessed on 17 October 2019).

44 Franz E. (2017). LEAD Innovation Management GmbH. April. www.lead-innovation.com/en.

45 Pfeffer J. (1994). *Competitive Advantage Through People*. Boston, MA: Harvard Business School Press.

46 Welch J. (1994). Quoted from '*Control Your Destiny or Someone Else Will.*' New York, NY: Harper Collins.

47 Duck J. D. (1995). *Leading Change: Why Transformation Efforts Fail, Managing Change—The Art of Balancing*. Boston, MA: Harvard Business School Publishing.

48 Tzu S. (2010). *The Art of War*. New York, NY: Delacorte Press.

49 Hultman. (1999). *Making Change Irresistible: Overcoming Resistance to Change in Your Organization*. Mumbai: Jairo Publishing House.

50 Prosci. (2016). *Best Practices in Change Management*. Fort Collins, CO: Prosci.

51 Conger J. A. & Kanungo R. N. (1988). The Empowerment Process: Integrating Theory and Practice. *Academy of Management Review* 13(3):471–482.

52 Jordan J. & Sorell M. (2019). Why You Should Create a 'Shadow Board' of Younger Employees. *Harvard Business Review*, June. https://hbr.org/2019/06/why-you-should-create-a-shadow-board-of-younger-employees (accessed on 17 October 2019).

53 Rick T. (2014). Change Management Is a Dolphin, Not a Whale. https://www.torbenrick.eu/blog/change-management/change-management-is-a-dolphin-not-a-whale/ (accessed on 6 October 2019).

54 Pareek U. (2002). *Effective Organizations: Beyond Management to Institution Building*. New Delhi: Oxford and IBH Publishing.

55 Maxwell J. C. (1999). *The 21 Irrefutable Laws of Leadership*. Mumbai: Magna Publishing.

56 Nadler D. A. (1995). *Beyond the Heroic Leader*. In *Discontinuous Change*. San Francisco, CA: Jossey-Bass.

57 Katzenbach J. R. (1996). Real Change Leaders. *Mckinsey Quarterly*, February. https://www.mckinsey.com/business-functions/organization/our-insights/real-change-leaders (accessed on 17 Ocotber 2019).

58 Kouzes J. M. & Posner B. Z. (2017). *The Leadership Challenge*. Delhi: Macmillan India.

59 Sanborn M. (2010). *Building Organization Change Capability: Beyond Change Management*. San Francisco, CA: Pfeiffer.

60 Lichtenstein S. (2012). The Role of Values in Leadership: How Leaders' Values Shape Value Creation. *Integral Leadership Review*, January. http://integralleadershipreview.com/6176-the-role-of-values-in-leadership-how-leaders-values-shape-value-creation/ (accessed on 17 October 2019).

61 Wilhelm W. (1996). *Learning from Past Leaders, in the Leader of the Future*. San Francisco, CA: Jossey-Bass.

62 Hurst D. K. (1995). *Crisis and Renewal: Meeting the Challenge of Organizational Change*. Boston, MA: Harvard Business School.

63 Tichy N. M. (1997). *The Leadership Engine*. New York, NY: Harper Collins.

64 Zohar D. (1997). *Tagore Memorial Oration*. Calcutta: Indian Institute of Management.

65 Zubin M. *Talentscapes* 3(1). Aon Hewitt. http://aonhewitt.co.in/Home/Resources/Talentscapes/Vol-3-Issue-1/Value-Based-Leadership (accessed on 6 October 2019).

66 Burns J. (1978). *Leadership*. New York, NY: Harper & Row.

67 Rajagopalachari C. (1963). *Our Culture*. Mumbai: Bhartiya Vidya Bhawan.

68 Hofstede G. (1980). *Cultural Consequences: International Difference in Work Related Values*. Beverly Hills, CA: SAGE Publications.

69 Lewis A. (1989). *To Thine Own Self Be True: The Relationship Between Spiritual Values and Emotional Health*. New York, NY: Main Street Books.

70 Roland A. (1987). The Familial Self – The Individual Self and The Transcendent Self: Psychoanalytic Reflections on India and America. *Psychoanalytic Review*, 74(2):239–252.

71 Krishna S. (1988). Developing Indigenous Strategies for Human Resource Development. *National HRD Network Newsletter*, 6–11.

72 Singh P. & Bhandarkar A. (1988). From Cultural Ethos to Organizational Milieu, *Indian Management*, October.

73 https://www.hofstede-insights.com/country-comparison/india/ (accessed on 17 October 2019).

74 Karp H. B. & Abramms B. (1992). Doing the Right Thing. *Training and Development Journal*, August:37–39.

75 https://www.tatasteel.com/corporate/pdf/TCOC.pdf (accessed on 17 October 2019).

76 Collins James C. & Porras Jerry I. (1996). Building Your Company's Vision. *Harvard Business Review*, September–October. https://hbr.org/1996/09/building-your-companys-vision?cm_sp=Article-_-Links-_-Comment (accessed on 17 October 2019).

77 Premji A. (2000). Leader for the Knowledge Ear. *Indian Management*, March.

78 Interview with Dr B. M. Munjal. *Smart Manager*, September-October 2009.

79 Manoharan M. D. & Jayaraman R. (1987). Value Orientation in Management Education, Workshop, Madurai, Kamraj University, February.

80 Chakraborty, S. K. (1991). *Management by Values*. Delhi: Oxford University Press.

81 Bennis W. (1989). *Why Leaders Can't Lead*. San Francisco, CA: Jossey-Bass.

82 Rao T. V. (2009). *Business Ethics and Professional Values*. New Delhi: Excel Books.

83 Barman H. (2009). Indian Ethos and Values in Modern Management. In *Excellence, Ethics and the World of Management*, eds. Ramesh K. Arora and Tanjul Saxena. Delhi: Alekh Publishers.

84 Capelli P., et al. (2010). Leadership Lessons from India. *Harvard Business Review*, March. https://hbr.org/2010/03/leadership-lessons-from-india (accessed on 17 October 2019).

85   Kanter R. M. (2009). Change Is the Hardest in the Middle. *Harvard Business Review*, August. https://hbr.org/2009/08/change-is-hardest-in-the-middl (accessed on 17 October 2019).

86   Cullen E. (2018). Change Management in the Digital Age. May. www.mentimeter.com.

87   Sharma S. K. (2019). Orbit Change. *Presentation in SHRM TechHR Conference*, Hyderabad, May.

About the Authors

Dr H. N. Arora

Dr H. N. Arora is an organization change specialist. He retired as Group Corporate Head HR and IR, Escorts Group, after having held top positions in Bhilwara group, Reliance, Indian Rayon and so on. He has closely observed the management philosophy of the founder of Reliance Group, late Sri Dhirubhai Ambani, in action. Dr Arora has helped many MSMEs and large industrial conglomerates in successful change management efforts, sometimes in seemingly hopeless situations. Subsequently, he did his doctorate on change management and leadership under Dr T. V. Rao.

Even now, Dr Arora continues as an adviser/consultant to many organizations. He is a keen observer of human collective behaviour, and a strong believer and practitioner of value-based leadership.

He is an enthusiastic student of Indic thought and philosophy.

Rajan Sinha

Rajan Sinha is the Chief Executive Officer, Mantrana Consulting. He is a PCC-level certified Life and Leadership Coach from Coach For-Life, Inc., USA. Formerly being the Head of Human Resources with many organizations such as HMT, Escorts (including Escorts Heart Institute), Denso India, OCM and so on, Rajan is an adviser, trainer and coach to many corporates and NGOs. He has also facilitated hundreds of workshops and training programmes in India, the Middle East and East Africa. He is one of the renowned psychometric assessors in India with the most international certification.

His other major works have been in the area of design and implementation of HR systems, policy making, team building and so on in India and abroad. He is also doing a fellowship at the Academy of Human Resource Development, Ahmedabad. He is a keen photographer and traveller.

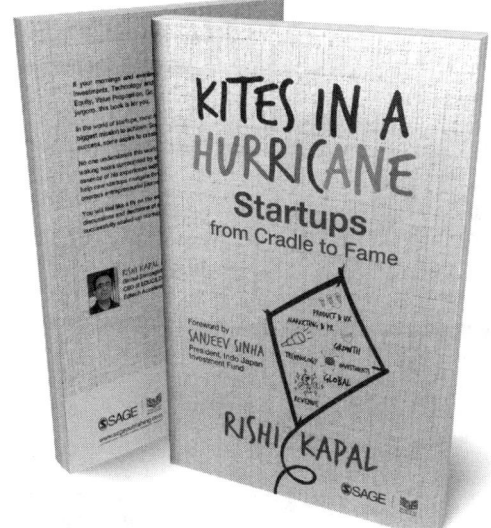